They That Sow In Tears
Coping with Grief Through Gardening

They That Sow In Tears
Coping with Grief Through Gardening

by

Catherine Chappell Lewis & Charles Nolan Sandifer

with Illustrations by Charles Nolan Sandifer

Published by The Master Design, Memphis, TN, USA

They That Sow In Tears – Coping With Grief Through Gardening
ISBN 1-930285-11-6

Published by The Master Design
   in cooperation with Master Design Ministries, Inc.
      PO Box 17865
      Memphis, TN 38187-0865
      bookinfo@masterdesign.org

Additional copies of this book may be purchased from www.masterdesign.org.

Printed in the USA by Evangel Press, Nappanee, Indiana.

JJ

Contents

Dedication

In memory of

Richard Sandifer
March 19, 1965 — February 3, 1996

and

Becky Lewis
June 22, 1978 — January 11, 1995

and in appreciation of

our spouses
Shirley Sandifer

Jim Lewis

and our children
Debbie Sandifer Bryant

Mimi Sandifer Hamilton

Brian Sandifer

Jay Lewis

Thomas Lewis

Acknowledgments

This special edition of *They That Sow In Tears – Coping With Grief Through Gardening*, authored by Catherine Lewis and Charles Sandifer in memory of their children, has been produced by Hospice of the River. We would like to express appreciation to them for allowing this edition of their book to be produced and allowing all proceeds from this edition to be contributed to the support of the children's grief camps of Trinity Hospice and Alliance Hospice, and the Hospice Memory Garden at the Memphis Botanical Gardens.

Hospice of the River was established in 1999 for the purpose of developing a residential hospice resource for the greater Memphis community. Laurel Reisman, first Board President, and Caby Byrne, Executive Director, were the founding agents of Hospice of the River. Operational funding for Hospice of the River was provided by grants from the Assisi Foundation, Church of the Holy Communion, United Way of Greater Memphis, and many individual contributions. In particular, Hospice of the River would like to recognize the significant memorials given in memory of Ben Reisman, husband, friend, and believer in the spirit of hospice care.

In appreciation for its leadership and direction, we would like to acknowledge the Board of Directors of the Hospice of the River for their work over a period of three years to develop and build a hospice residence for Memphis. Though the decision was made in early 2002 to discontinue the current plans for the residence, it is our hope and dream that the seeds which were sown in these three years will one day lead to the reality of a hospice residence for Memphis.

Laurel Reisman
Caby Byrne

To the Reader

The Sandifers and the Lewises have been friends for about 30 years. They have shared many interests: music, gardening, teaching each other's children, playing pranks, and volunteering in church. Like all good friends eventually do, they have also shared heartache.

Richard Sandifer was diagnosed with juvenile (type 1) diabetes in 1978 at age 13. His was always a "brittle" (hard to control) case. At age 27, his situation was further complicated by lupus. In spite of his health problems, he earned a bachelor's degree in history and entered the University of Memphis Law School. But from 1993 to 1996, he spent half of his time in the hospital and half of that time in the Intensive Care Unit (ICU).

Tenth-grader Becky Lewis had never had a serious illness in her life, but in December 1993, her world was shattered. She came down with what promised to be a routine, treatable pneumonia. However, on Christmas Eve, her father rushed her to the hospital, where she stopped breathing and was put on a respirator. The Sandifers came to share the time in the ICU waiting room.

Becky rallied, and for a while it looked as if she would recover. In the ICU she could play musical requests on her electric keyboard, win games of "Boggle" with the recreation therapist, and even do leg-lifts in bed, but she could not get away from that respirator. Several times during Becky's year of "two steps forward, three steps back," Richard was also hospitalized. So whenever the Sandifers and the Lewises saw each other in the hospital, the first question was whether they were there socially, or "on business too."

Both Becky and Richard were put on waiting lists for organ transplants, and their families shared the hopes and concerns associated with that. But, neither Becky nor Richard survived long enough to receive the needed organs. Becky lost her fight for life January 11, 1995, and Richard lost his February 3, 1996.

Since then, both families have done what most do. They have attempted to carry on. After one musical performance, a friend said, "Just like old times." No, nothing is really like old times, but they do manage to share laughs again, as well as the sadness.

They each found comfort working in their gardens and frequently compared notes. They also began to notice that planting a memory garden was often a universal response to grief. As they continued to find consolation in their gardening, they wanted to share their love of gardening with others.

Most garden books begin with analyzing your site, studying your climate, evaluating the relative merits of particular plants, and diagramming your plan. Usually a good amount of time is spent with measuring tape and graph paper before the spade touches dirt. Generally that is a good approach, but if you have recently lost a loved one by death, you will probably find that too tedious. This is one time when you should act now and think later. Whenever the urge hits you, put this book down and go outside to begin your garden.

The Sandifers and Lewises have a lot to tell you about people like you who have planted beautiful tributes to their loved ones, and they want to give you good advice to help you establish a garden that will give you pleasure and comfort. The most important goal, however, is to get you outdoors into the healing activity of gardening. Their wish for you is that "They that sow in tears shall reap in joy" (Psalm 126:5, ASV).

Chapter 1
<u>Grief and Gardening</u>

How can a garden help me?

Listen to Tom: "...As I dug, the feelings flowed through me: the sadness of missing him, the gratefulness of having been his son, and the anger and frustration of my powerlessness. All of these feelings found their way into this hole. The act of digging became an avenue for the various thoughts and feelings to arise."[1]

And to Rucy: "You put your feet on the ground, and it's solid... When you're feeling sad...when you're feeling unbalanced or you're feeling kind of lifeless... just to go sit in it, is healing."[2]

And to Earl: "I hadn't started my garden yet, so I went out there and dug a great big hole. I mean I just went out and kept on working out there in the yard to get rid of my frustration. I filled the hole back in again and then I dug another. That seemed to help."[3]

It seems to help. When you can't find the words, or no one seems willing to listen, a garden can help you express your feelings.

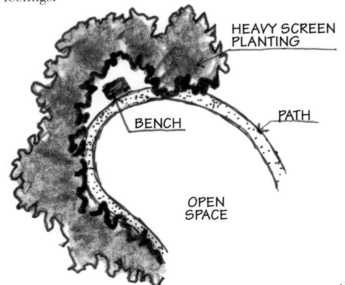

HEAVY SCREEN PLANTING

BENCH

PATH

OPEN SPACE

People may ask, "What phase of grief are you in now?" (referring to five or six neatly ordered stages of mourning). But the term "phase" often oversimplifies the path of your pain. Stages of grief often overlap and repeat, without clear endpoints. Like a weed-choked path, grief might go straight ahead, but more often it doubles back or leads off to sidetracks. You seem to lose your way and may have to retrace some steps to get back to the main path. Here are some of the emotional stops along that path, some that you may visit more than once. For many people, gardening helps with many of these emotions.

"I feel so numb"

The funeral is over. It was a difficult but busy time. There were people to call, arrangements to make, and other activities that at least gave you something constructive to do. Now the out-of-town relatives have gone home, and friends have returned to their schedules. A strange, stunned quiet settles over you.

Now, what do you do? People have told you that "time heals all wounds". You don't see how that's possible, but you feel you might as well start doing something to pass that time. What is there to do that would seem normal and sane but not mentally taxing?

Gardening provides some wonderfully mechanical, mindless tasks with varying levels of physical exertion. It allows you to get caught up in the soothing rhythm of digging, raking, trimming shrubs, pulling weeds or hosing down the lawn (even if you have a sprinkler system). It gives your mind a chance to run along whatever avenue it needs to try to sort out the confusing things that have happened.

Your first task in preparing a garden flower bed is to dig up and discard a section of the lawn. Whatever time of year it is, notice the remnants of the previous season and signs of the next one. Even in some of the early days in a garden, as you dig, you may find yourself contemplating the cycle of nature and seeing yourself and your loved ones as a part of that cycle. The Bible tells us: "For everything there is a season...A time to be born, and a time to die; a time to plant, and a time to pluck up that which is planted."[4]

Isaiah 40:6-8 says: "All flesh is grass...The grass withers...the flower fades...but the word of our God will stand for ever."[5] These thoughts may bring a sad smile or cause bitter tears to flow. Either way, it helps.

"It's so lonely to mourn"

Our culture sometimes fails us in time of grief. An opinion survey once reported that the man on the street thinks it should take somewhere between 48 hours and two weeks to recover from a significant loss! This is in contrast to clinical studies, which say that 18 months to two years is not unusual.[6]

So when you see the uncomfortable looks on your friends' faces, and they urge you not to cry, you yearn for refuge that is solitary, but not lonely.

While loneliness can permeate a solitary room, it seldom stays within a garden. In a garden, the living, progressive rhythms of plants and the background noises of birds and other animals give you a sense of companionship without invasion. If other gardeners are working nearby, you can feel a partnership or kinship, but you don't have to say anything.

Many feel closest to the Creator while taking part in the creative work of gardening. You may not feel much like talking to Him at this point, but as the Master Gardener, He will work by your side without requiring you to speak. One bereaved mother said, "As I worked, I found myself thinking of Gethsemane, the garden where Jesus prayed for strength to endure the cross. Many times in my garden, I have hummed the rich, deep, sad melody that Handel composed for the text, 'He was despised and rejected, a man of sorrows and acquainted with grief,'[7] and I have wept with the realization that I was not alone."

"I just wish I could tear something up!"

"When I lost my son Donald at [age] eleven, I tore up the whole front yard, and all the lawn went. I was out there like a mad woman with a spade, just tearing up the lawn, sitting down in the dirt, digging away and getting rid of it. I guess it was a creative way to get rid of hurt and anger..."[8]

Nothing beats gardening for releasing all that pent up frustration and emotion. Stab the earth, murder some weeds, and uproot the shrub that gets in your way. Most new projects begin with some constructive destruction. As you swing that ax or stomp on the spade, you can ask, "Why?!" as long as you need to.

Paula[9] began her project during the different sort of grief of a divorce. "Since it was winter, the weather was awful, the ground was saturated, and the nurseries were bare, there was no choice but to go into demolition mode. I ripped. I tore. I violated. I was well suited to the task — I had tons of nervous energy and no life to speak of."

How dare that unwanted plant thrive when your loved one has died? What gives it the right to live? Of course, it sounds irrational to think that, but go ahead and vent your anger at an offending weed. It's better than ranting at other bereaved family members.

In *Chicken Soup for the Mother's Soul*, Jeanne White says: "It seems to me every weed I pull is a bit of grief I am learning to set aside, a tear I've weeded out so that good cheer can grow again."[10]

We've even thought it might be a good idea to put one invasive plant somewhere in your garden to give you weed-pulling therapy for years to come!

"It's my fault. Why didn't I do things differently?"

Many people feel some degree of guilt or regret. Often these feelings are totally without basis, but sometimes they are valid. Either way, there is usually nothing that can be changed. Whether the guilt is real or imagined, toiling in your garden can feel like some form of penance. This feeling can be even stronger when the garden is dedicated to the memory of the one who has died.

"I feel so helpless"

"Why wasn't I able to do something to prevent this?" Gardening can teach you the balance between things that are not in your control and things that are. You can't control how many rainy days your garden receives, but you can provide good drainage or extra water. You can't influence when the last spring frost will come, but you can plan around it for the best possible timing of blooms.

In a garden, nature teaches you gently that some things are beyond your control.

You make mistakes in the garden, and this plant or that suffers for your ignorance or neglect. Still the garden forgives you, favoring you with other successes, and gradually you learn to forgive yourself.

Every garden produces some successes, even for the most inexperienced among us. The steady progression of the plants toward maturity assures you that there is order in Creation after all. There is a feeling of control that comes from digging a hole and saying, "This plant will go here." You have a say-so in this small corner of the world, your garden. As Charles Warner said, "However small [your garden] is on the surface, it is four thousand miles deep; and that is a very handsome property."[11]

"Quit trying to cheer me up"

Do you sometimes resent those well-meaning people who try to help you "look at the bright side"? What bright side? Don't they know that sometimes you just need to mope? The writer of Proverbs certainly knew this: "Like one who takes away a garment on a cold day, or like vinegar poured on soda, is one who sings songs to a heavy heart."[12]

Mourning is a necessary part of grief. Some of your friends will have the sensitivity to know when you need to cry and when you need a break from mourning. A garden is one of those friends:

> "She never said, 'cease to grieve,'
> but she grieved with me,
> and, for the first time
> — I felt I was not alone."[13]

A garden's pleasures are subtle, gently lifting your spirits. The silky softness of a pastel flower petal, the gentle breeze on your face, the activity of a bee at work, or the warm sunshine on your arms can begin to persuade you that maybe there is some good left in the world.

"How can I just 'get on with life'?"

A garden is not a quick fix, like a television show where every problem is resolved in 30 minutes (minus commercial time). The gentle, natural pace of the plant world stands in contrast to the rush of our modern media culture to "get on with your life."

Don't try to race through your grief recovery. Some weed killers work by forcing abnormally rapid growth, so that the unwanted plant literally dies of exhaustion. Often, the fast track isn't beneficial for people or plants.

A garden gradually offers cheer and healing. You can influence a plant's growth in some ways. You may prune to make it bushier, and fertilize to make it more vigorous, but you cannot make a plant grow faster than God intended.

The Cree Indians of North America practiced a ritual symbolizing the gradual healing of grief. The mourner selected a tree and, after praying, stripped off a piece of the bark. This "wounded tree" served as a living symbol of the hurt in the mourner's heart. As the seasons passed and the tree healed, it was a visible reminder of the person's slow but certain healing.

"I'm not really interested in anything"

Sometimes you need to retreat for a while, but withdrawing completely into a shell for too long is unhealthy. If you can manage that first step of deciding to plant a garden, the project will coax you into taking an interest in your surroundings. You begin to notice others' gardens, or something in the garden center attracts your curiosity. For a moment the fog lifts, and a twinge of life comes through. It's a start.

Mention your project to a gardening friend, and you are sure to get some plants delivered to your door. You may want to sit in a darkened room today, but you know that tomorrow those plants are counting on you to put them in a viable spot. That sense of responsibility can be just the right nudge to get you moving. You don't need to have great demands placed on you, but you do need something to live for.

Kate Cunningham, a painter in Indianapolis, nurtures a rooftop garden that she and her late husband began. "I didn't paint for two years after Jim died, but I could still garden. Some days it was a real chore to get out and water and take care of the plants, but I had to. I couldn't just let the garden die, too."[15]

Nothing can replace the person you have lost, but recognition of your need to nurture can help. "I think the saddest thing was that I still wanted to be a mother. I had all this love of mothering in me, and what better way to mother — go into the garden. Go into the garden and tend plants."[16] You crave that lost touch. The garden is palpable. You can touch it, see it, smell it, and do for it — a need that is part of your grief.

"What's wrong with my family?"

No matter how close and loving your family is, each individual will have to grieve in his own way. You will not be able to share completely in each other's grief. There will be times when you're unable to provide the support that the others want from you, and they won't be capable of helping you the way you wish they would. Accept this fact, and it will take a lot of the strain off family relationships during this time.

Working together and individually on a gardening project can help the family share and express their feelings. Children often prefer not to visit the cemetery where their grief might normally be discussed. A memory garden provides a setting where you can naturally talk about the good memories and the loss. Give the children some input into what is planted. When you get suggestions like "Aw, please, she would think it was funny to have a jalapeño pepper in the garden," you could either incorporate the idea or decide to give each child an area of his own.

"Heaven seems so far away"

Even when we believe strongly that we will be reunited with loved ones in heaven, death brings that frustrating lack of being able to touch and see and hold. There's an aching desire to remain somehow connected. For Stu Upchurch, the statue of a little cherub with a bird in his hand is representative of baby Jason. The cherub, surrounded by blue and white flowers, looks into the house from his place on the terrace and helps Stu to visualize the real Jason smiling down on him from heaven.

Your garden provides something for those senses that can no longer be stimulated by your loved one. You might select plants with tangible traits that can represent intangible ones — a sweet fragrance, a bright color, the vigor of a spreading vine.

Gardening is an optimistic occupation. You cultivate the ground, plant seeds, water them, stand back, and generally expect to see green shoots coming up from the ground after a while. The Bible uses this image to illustrate the promise of life after death. The seed must "die" in order to achieve new life as a fruitful plant.[17] The patience that we learn through our gardening is the same kind of patience we must develop in waiting to see our loved ones again. "See how the farmer waits for the land to yield its valuable crop and how patient he is for the autumn and spring rains. You, too, be patient and stand firm, because the Lord's coming is near."[18]

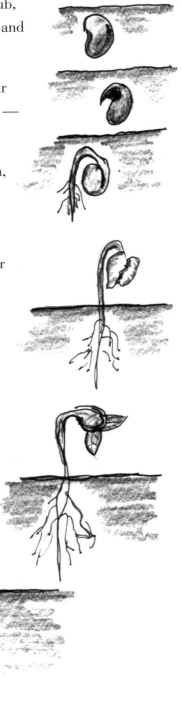

Chapter 2
Memory Gardens

How many times have you said, "I wish I could still do something for her," or "I'm doing this because he would have liked it"? We arrange the nicest funeral we can afford and keep flowers on the grave, but it isn't very satisfying. So you clean her room, iron his clothes, and still catch yourself trying to buy gifts or to prepare favorite meals for that someone who has gone far away.

Is there any way to satisfy that need? To feel that we're still doing something for a loved one who has been taken away from us by death? Do those beyond the grave somehow know what we are doing and still care? Whether you believe they do or not, planting a memory garden can work as a way for you to honor your loved one.

Significance

When Timothy McVeigh bombed the Murrah Federal Building in Oklahoma City, his actions said, "These people don't matter. They're unimportant." Immediately people around the country responded with their own actions saying, "Yes, they did matter. They were all individuals with hopes and dreams. They were worthy of respect, and we will honor them."

Employees at the Social Security Administration headquarters in Baltimore funded a memorial garden including the state flowers of Oklahoma and Maryland to symbolize the link between the two groups of employees. Texas Garden Clubs hosted a Community Remembrance Day at Texas A&M and planted an Aristocrat pear tree, whose pure, white blossoms would always remind them of the innocent children who had died. The memorial garden in Oklahoma City includes 168 empty chairs with a victim's name on each one to remind people that these were individuals, not statistics.

When you give your time and your money to create a memory garden, whether it is a special place in your own yard or a public place, your actions announce "Here was someone who was worthy of honor."

Beauty

Out of the ugliness of death, people crave beauty and peace. What a great gift you give when you can take an unappealing section of land and transform it into a place of beauty. Sallie Williamson[1] did this at the Presbyterian church cemetery in Concord, North Carolina. It had been overgrown with briers and weeds before she converted it into a garden in memory of her mother, Adeline Phifer. Since 1930 the garden has bloomed with azaleas, dogwoods, magnolias, spring bulbs, and summer annuals, causing the name of Adeline Phifer to always be associated with beauty.

Helping others

Obviously, if your garden is a gift to the community, you help others, but your backyard garden can be a benevolent memorial as well. With us as the agent, our loved one is still able to do good deeds. It gives him or her a degree of immortality on this earth.

Buy your plants from a local charity (see Chart 2.1). For example, the Baddour Center in Senatobia, Mississippi, is a residential school for adults with developmental problems. Part of their income is generated by greenhouses operated by the residents. Gardeners have the opportunity to help the school and to obtain very fine quality plants at the same time.

Becky Lewis had been impressed when the Center's outstanding choir, "The Miracles," had sung at her elementary school. Years later when her mother Catherine bought some Baddour plants for her memorial "Becky Garden," she knew Becky would have been pleased.

For vegetable gardeners, the Garden Writers Association of America[2] suggests "Plant a Row for the Hungry." Plant an

extra row in your garden and donate its produce to charities like Second Harvest, soup kitchens or food banks in your community. Dedicate that row in your loved one's memory, and help it to flourish.

Your garden may provide an oasis for others. Thomas Hicks' Aunt Mae[3] suffered the loss of her husband and her only child in less than a year. She had to move to a smaller home, but it had a big yard where she planted a garden. Thomas enjoyed his visits to the garden, sitting with his aunt under the beech tree. It was not until her death that he realized he was only one of many who were quietly encouraged and nurtured during their garden visits with Aunt Mae.

Living On

One of our biggest fears is that people will forget. It seems that forgetting steals more life away from our loved one. As plants in your garden multiply, you may be able to pass along their offspring to friends who will treasure them as a memento. This insures that, even if your own gardening efforts eventually fall by the wayside, some seed of memory will live on.

The Rubertinos[4] reach a large group of people in an effort to salvage some meaning from their tragedy. Little Vincent was killed at age four by a drunk driver. The sunflower that he had started in a paper cup at preschool grew to over eight feet and produced enough seed for a garden of sunflowers the following year. Now when the Rubertinos share their story, they also share the sunflower seeds for their listeners to plant as a reminder.

Plants that your loved one cared for can be shared with children and grandchildren. Besides her roses, Elizabeth Gooch had an azalea that was a souvenir from a trip to Bellengrath Gardens. When Elizabeth died, her daughter Beth moved the azalea and some of the roses to her own house. Tending these plants helped Beth feel that she was still doing something for her mother. It continued the legacy and encouraged a feeling that something of her mother remained with her.

Cemetery flowers

Audrey Roberts didn't know how she could return to gardening after her father passed away. They had enjoyed so many hours of father-daughter companionship as he sat in his chair and watched her tend their flowers. She dreaded going back out to the garden alone.

But the roses bloomed especially well the first year after his death, enough for her to carry bouquets to her parents' graves and to share with the neighbors too. You may have heard stories of expatriates who asked that a little soil from their homeland be scattered on their graves. Flowers from home carry those same sentiments.

Symbolism

You can construct your garden in a way that reflects the personality of the person you have lost. Be as sentimental as you like. Choose brightly colored flowers to reflect her cheerful personality, a vigorous plant to symbolize his energy, or soft moss to express her tenderness. Select accessories such as statuary, bird feeders, or wind chimes, which will serve as reminders.

If your loved one had a terrific sense of humor, by all means, let your garden reflect that. When MIT student Christina Park died, her friends reminisced about the time that she had colored her hair orange. They suggested planting a garden of orange flowers in her memory.

Naturally, if your loved one had a special gardening interest, you may want to build upon that. Perry Morgan financed the wildflower meadow at the Norfolk (Virginia) Botanical Garden in memory of his wife Bunny. She was a wildflower enthusiast and would have enjoyed the 50 species along the garden's paths and near its fountain and gazebo.

Members of Northminster Baptist Church in Jackson, Mississippi, knew that Rev. Barbara Oliver had loved daffodils, so they planted hundreds of bulbs around the church as a memorial to her. Each year the yellow blossoms come up to help blot out sad memories of her illness and to remind the congregation of Barbara's new life after death.

Some people have designed gardens around Biblical plants[5] or plants mentioned in works of literature.[6] Others have been attracted to plant names that suggest particular hobbies, vocations or interests (see Charts 2.2 and 2.3). Your garden is a personal statement of who you are and the individual you are honoring.

Namesake plants

Did you know that there is probably a plant somewhere with your loved one's name? A popular pink hyacinth is named Anne Marie. There is a pink dianthus named Helen and a red azalea named Emily. If your loved one shared the name of the late Princess of Wales, you can plant a Diana hibiscus, a Diana carnation, a Diana tulip, a Diana rose…

Although there are more flowers named for women, there are still many named for men too: a red daylily named Jay, a white phlox named David, and a blue Siberian iris named Walter, to mention a few.[7]

How did all these plants get their names? People like you gained the expertise to develop the plants, earning the privilege of naming them. Fenwick Chappell (an orchid hobbyist and father of co-author Catherine Chappell Lewis) was given an American Orchid Society award for a pink orchid that he cloned. That orchid and its descendants carry the official name Dendrobium Nestor 'Laura' AM/AOS/CCM, for his late daughter, Laura. If there isn't a plant with your loved one's name, you may be able to develop one, or watch the garden catalogs for new varieties that come out every year.

Favorite things

Amy Petty, who survived the bombing in Oklahoma City, planted a garden that her lost coworkers would have liked.[8] Each flower was selected to represent a specific coworker. Among them are daffodils for Claudette, who had wanted to plant some in her own yard, irises for Robbin, who always brought some to work when hers were in bloom and azaleas for Kathy, who had assured Amy that they were easy to grow. Kim had mentioned that her windflowers were in bloom, so Amy planted windflowers in her memory. Sonja had joked that her bright yellow dress made her look like a big sunflower, so Amy planted a hybrid sunflower — coincidentally, named "Sonja."

Amy learned more about her friends' preferences for colors and kinds of plants when she talked to their relatives. Jamie's mother said she loved yellow roses. Victoria's mother contributed some pink cannas from her daughter's yard. As her garden grows Amy sends pictures of the flowers to her friends' families to let them know that she remembers and shares their loss.

Life

A garden is an appropriate memorial because it is alive and dynamic. It hurts us that the person who died is now frozen in time, never to get any taller, never to learn any new skills and never to develop new relationships. But a garden is always growing and changing. It embodies that life that your loved one had and still has beyond our sight. Perhaps the only drawback to a garden as a memorial is that it is not permanent, but even this reminds us that life is fragile and transient. The more permanent a memorial is, the more lifeless it is. So if you want to commemorate a person's death, build a stone obelisk, but if you want to celebrate his life, plant a garden.

Chart 2.1

Sample Listing of Plant Sales Benefiting Memphis and Mississippi nonprofit organizations

- Wildflower Plant Sale at Dixon Gallery and Gardens
- Plant Sale at Memphis Zoo
- Memphis Botanic Gardens Plant Sales
- Lichterman Nature Center Plant Sales
- Geranium Sale by Memphis Chapter of Zonta Clubs International
  (80% of proceeds in a typical year went to Hope House for HIV-affected children)
- Baddour Center for developmentally challenged adults, Senatobia MS
- Memphis Jewish Home Plant Sale (to help establish a garden in memory of
  Holocaust victims and in honor of survivors)
- Temple Israel Tulip Bulb Sale

Chart 2.2

Examples of Plants with Musical Names

Company	Species	Variety
Van Bourgondien	Dahlia	"Cha-cha"
Van Bourgondien	Caladium	"Pink Symphony"
Van Bourgondien	Dahlia	"Duet"
Van Bourgondien	Tall phlox	"Tenor"
Van Bourgondien	Canterbury bells	
Van Bourgondien	Coral Bells	
Van Bourgondien	Virginia bluebells	
Burpee	Dahlia mix	"Rigoletto"
Burpee	Oriental poppy mix	"Pizzicato"
Burpee	Bells of Ireland	
Burpee	Marigold mix	"Disco"
Burpee	New Guinea impatiens	"Tango"
Burpee	Hybrid geranium	"Applause"

Sources: Spring 1997 Retail Catalog. Van Bourgondien Bros., 245 Route 109, P.O. Box 1000, Babylon, NY 11702-9004
Burpee Gardens 1997 catalog. W. Atlee Burpee & Co., 300 Park Avenue, Warminster, PA 18991-0001.

Chart 2.3

Categories of Interest and Corresponding Plant Types

Interest	Company	Variety
Military	Monrovia	Butterfly Bush:Black Knight
		Camellia: Colonel Firey
Geography	Monrovia	Potentilla: Mount Everest
		Mandevilla: Chilean Jasmine
States	Monrovia	Azalea: Alaska
		Redbud: Oklahoma
Royalty	Monrovia	Rose: Sir Thomas Lipton
		Ceanothus: Victoria
Nautical	Monrovia	Phlox: White Admiral
		Rhododendron: Blue Ensign
History/Politics	Van Bourgondien	Daffodil: Winston Churchill
		Tulip: General Eisenhower

Chapter 3
Establishing Your First Garden

Starting a memory garden is really very simple. There are only three basic steps:

1. Prepare a spot.
2. Plant or place something there.
3. Make a note of it.

Don't be intimidated or paralyzed by trying to do a perfect job. Follow your heart at the beginning, and logic can catch up later. Unlike the landscape professional whose client is paying to have the job done "right" the first time, you are free to learn as you go, to change your mind about what you like, and to experience the joy of discovery as most amateur gardeners do. Later we can describe some principles that will help you understand why you like the appearance of some things better than others, but first:

Prepare a spot

Pick an obvious spot for planting. The most important thing is that the place is convenient for you. Can you enjoy seeing it from your kitchen or bedroom window? Is it visible from your porch or driveway? If you prefer a secluded place, is it still easily accessible to you?

You might choose the ground surrounding your terrace, a plot next to the house, or an area beneath a tree. Jackie Bridges planted "Mom's garden" near the entrance to her garage. Reminding her of her mother, the little bed of flowers sends Jackie off in the morning and greets her return each evening.

It might be possible to choose a location that was special to your loved one. Cy Robinson's family helped his elementary school build a baseball field in memory of their athletic son. At the entrance is a marker proclaiming it "Cy's Field." Friends enjoy the flowers planted around the base of the marker although they know that Cy would hardly notice if he were racing to the field.

Once you've chosen the place, tear up the soil. Digging and turning the earth and then digging and turning some more allows a wonderful release of emotions,

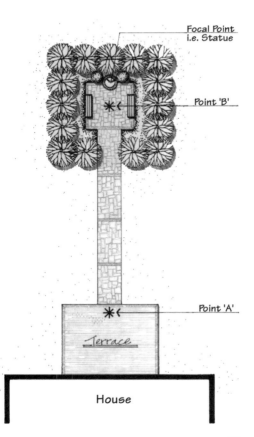

and the plants will thank you for the well-cultivated bed. Add some compost or other organic matter. This helps loosen heavy clay soils and provides better water retention in sandy soils. If you are starting with a small, manageable site, it's easy to buy bags of humus, vermiculite, topsoil, or other products. A dash of slow-release commercial fertilizer helps too. Once you have loosened the bed, try to avoid walking on it and packing it back down.

Get something to plant

Now go to a garden center and pick out something that strikes your fancy. The advantages to using your local garden center instead of a catalog are threefold: you won't have to wait for shipment, most of their stock will be appropriate

The plaque at the entrance to Cy's Field includes an engraving of Cy Robinson's picture and the Scripture verse from 2 Timothy 4:7, "I have fought the good fight, I have finished the race, I have kept the faith."

to your climate, and you can get advice. Sometimes you even make a new friend. Catalog shopping has its own set of rewards, but for now, take the hands-on, person-to-person approach of the local garden center.

You may be attracted to a particular plant for no obvious reason, or something about it might suggest a connection to your loved one. It may be a favorite color or the name of a plant that appeals to you. Plant varieties come with all sorts of names like "My Love...Bleeding Heart...Valentine...First Kiss" or "Little Miss Muffet...Red Riding Hood... Pinnochio...Snow White."

Notice which types of plants the garden center stocks in large quantity. Make your selections in similar proportions to theirs. If they are planning to sell thousands of one type of plant, they know it's been proven to grow well in your area.

20

If they have only a few specimens of something that intrigues you, buy just a sample to plant among the more common varieties.

During your digging, you probably noticed whether you were working in hot sunlight, cool shade, or a combination of the two. This information can guide you toward plants that will work better for you. Nursery plants usually have tags that include information on light requirements. You'll also notice that good garden centers display their plants with the proper light levels to keep them healthy for sale. Shop in the open sunlight for sun-worshipping plants, and head for the light-filtering canopy to find shade-loving plants.

Gifts are a source of plants as well. You may be able to use the potted azalea that someone sent you at the time of the funeral (although plants forced into bloom for florists' use may not always adapt to the garden). Some of the houseplants can take up temporary residence in your garden during mild weather. Gardening friends will offer you plants when they hear about your project. Try not to feel bad if you can't use all that they give you, but enjoy the ones you can. These can serve as a reminder of the kindness of others.

Other plants come to you as "legacy plants" or "heirloom plants." When Audrey Rainey sold her mother's house, she moved many of the lilies and ferns from her mother's garden to her own. She also added lots of the flowers that bear her mother's name, Pansy. Charles even transplanted a crape myrtle tree from his grandparents' house in Louisiana, not once, but a second time when he moved. You may be able to obtain seeds from the four o'clock bush at your aunt's house, daffodil bulbs from your grandmother's home, or cuttings from the "sweetheart rose" that grew in your teacher's yard. Heirloom plants contribute to a sense of continuity in life when you need it most.

Notice the plants you see around town. Did you like that eye-catching bed of blue, yellow and red at the bank yesterday?

Symbols for Light on Nursery Labels

◯ Full Sun (sunlight for at least 6 hours/day)

● Shade

◖ Combination

Were you attracted to the white flowering shrub you saw next to the office building? Maybe those little plants with the big red flowers will work at your house too. Someone at the garden center can probably tell you what they are and make suggestions for their planting and care. Don't worry about how things "fit in." If you think a particular plant will give you enjoyment, give it a try.

You may wonder whether you should buy seeds or nursery plants. The second year, there is a lot to be said for seeds. They are much less expensive, and serve as a beautiful parable of resurrection. The first year of the garden, however, indulge yourself with the instant beauty of nursery plants. Buy short, compact seedlings that are healthier than older ones that have become spindly. Small annuals will hurry to produce lots of bloom in one season.

Get more than one kind of plant. Use anything you like, but don't commit your whole project to one specimen that might not thrive. Buying a variety is insurance that, if you are unlucky with one thing, you will succeed with others. Gardening is often an adventure of trial and error, and most gardeners wouldn't have it any other way, but hedge your bets. Diversify your garden portfolio.

Susan and Rick Callaway learned the hard way that you should plant a variety. When they lost a baby by miscarriage, they planted a single Bradford pear tree in their yard as a memorial. In short order, their two very young, very active children broke the little tree down to the ground. Susan grieved for the tree and realized that, in her mind, it had come to represent the baby. She was also furious at the two children for their carelessness, and she felt guilty for being angry at them. Fortunately, the next year Emily was born, and the tree managed to put up new growth almost as if it sensed the new baby's arrival. Susan might have been spared the extra grief, however, if she and Rick had planted a small flower bed with the young sapling as just one part of the overall plan.

Choose something to place

The first thing that attracts your interest may not even be a plant. A garden bench or trellis may appeal to you. You may want to begin with a hummingbird feeder and surround it with red flowers that will also lure the tiny birds. For Stu, the cherub statue came first. Later he surrounded it with white flowers to represent heaven and blue ones for his little boy Jason.

Consider building around something that is already in place like a tree stump, something stationary with a sense of strength about it. A seat or any substantial object that you can lean on helps give a sense of stability in a world that has just careened crazily out of control.

Write it down

The third step is to write down what you have done. This is helpful to any gardener but especially important to one in mourning, when absent-mindedness can be such a vexing problem. You don't want to start digging next spring in a "bare" spot that is actually home to some sleeping perennials that you forgot.

There are many approaches to keeping a garden journal. Adapt the one that works best for you. You might buy a loose leaf notebook or a card file, or treat yourself to a bound blank book with flowers on the cover. A few gardeners try to use their computers.

The computer can be a useful tool. You can record all sorts of details like planting dates, blooming times, sizes of plants, purchase information, color of flowers, and anything else that you could also write in a journal. The unique benefit of the computer is that, with a database program, you can sort your entries according to any category you wish. Will a certain pink flower clash with that orange one nearby? Your computer can sort your list by color and bloom time to see if the two plants will be in bloom simultaneously or if one will be a quiet green when the other is blooming.

A simple journal method allows one page or one index card for each kind of plant you use. Then you can add notes about the plant's performance over the months and years. Another option is to record garden activities in diary form. Daily notes are not necessary, but you will find it useful to record events like planting dates, unusual weather, and appearance of

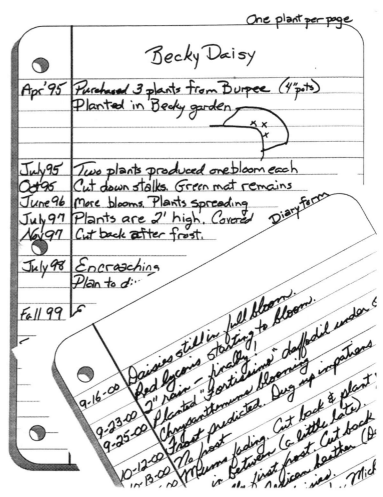

new plant growth. Your notes may be so brief that they fit on a monthly calendar, but most people find that they need more space for comments and sketches.

If all this overwhelms you, and record-keeping is a task you simply cannot tolerate, at least make a sketch or photograph of your garden and keep plant markers and seed packets in a shoebox somewhere! Whatever method you choose, looking back over the record of what you planted those first seasons will help you see your own progress, as well as the development of your garden.

One more thing: Keep your options open

Decisions will come more easily if you know they can be reversed. In laying out beds or building garden structures, do not hurry to establish permanence. Most features that don't involve concrete or mortared brick can be dismantled or moved without great difficulty.

If you use landscape timbers, wait until next year to nail them together. You can stack two rows overlapping, and they will be sturdy enough for now. You may choose railroad ties, although they are heavier to move than landscape timbers. You can also edge beds with mortar-free stone walls known as dry stack. These can be quite permanent but will also be no problem to dismantle if you decide that you want another arrangement.

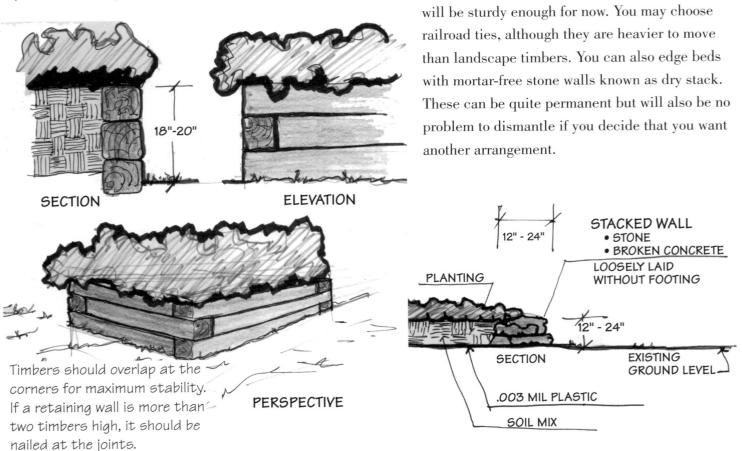

SECTION   18"-20"

ELEVATION

PERSPECTIVE

Timbers should overlap at the corners for maximum stability. If a retaining wall is more than two timbers high, it should be nailed at the joints.

STACKED WALL
• STONE
• BROKEN CONCRETE

LOOSELY LAID WITHOUT FOOTING

12" - 24"

PLANTING

SECTION

12" - 24"

EXISTING GROUND LEVEL

.003 MIL PLASTIC

SOIL MIX

If you want to have a walkway in your garden, you might use only stepping stones the first year so that you can be sure the route is a natural one. One season of stumbling into the flowerbed will tell you that the location of the path needs adjustment. Mulch is another excellent material for a temporary pathway because it can be turned under if you decide later that the place would be better for something else.

You can even build a terrace that is solid, yet moveable. A common method is to set bricks or pavers in a smooth bed of sand and sweep additional sand between the bricks instead of using mortar. It's semi-permanent, but you can remove the bricks and dig the sand into the soil if you change your mind.

Upright structures like trellises often need to be set in concrete, but you may be able to anchor them temporarily with stakes until you are sure they are where you want them. If you envision a vine-covered arbor, preview the effect by planting it with an annual climber, such as morning glory or cardinal climber. Next year when you know it's what you want, you can set it in concrete and plant your climbing rose or perennial vine.

Your first effort doesn't need to be a masterpiece but only something that will give you satisfaction. It may take years to develop your own philosophy of gardening and to acquire expert knowledge, but it only takes a shovel, some dirt, and a few seeds to become a "real gardener."

Trellises can lend support to perennial climbers including climbing roses and vines like clematis, ivy, cross vine, and Virginia creeper. Annual vines include cardinal climber, cypress vine, morning glory, and some gourds.

Chapter 4
A Garden for Rachel As Told by Marian Sinn

Our beautiful, tall, dark-eyed, smiling Rachel died at home on August 8, 1995, at the age of 16 from an astrocytoma brain tumor.

On August 19, during a hot, sunny afternoon, more than 200 relatives and friends gathered to bury Rachel's ashes at the little Anglican church just down the road. A day after the funeral, I became obsessed with the urge to "bring Rachel home." My husband Hans and I talked about various ways we could do this. We weren't even sure if we could simply dig up the urn. We consulted with legal and Church authorities and became certain that it was neither illegal nor irreverent to dig up the urn and move it.

We quickly began to think about putting the urn in a special place in the garden, but nothing seemed just right. I favored a little clearing just on the other side of the driveway, where Rachel's garden statue of St. Francis stands. When I came home from work one afternoon, Hans walked me a few steps past St. Francis, through the cedar and the sumac, where the land slopes down and is open. It caught my imagination immediately. It was the perfect place for a small sunken garden — slightly hidden, but very accessible.

One of Rachel's older brothers, Nick, is a landscape technician. He and Hans threw themselves into the project. After they had agreed on a basic design, a neighbor came with a backhoe and scooped out the slope to about four feet deep and 22 x 22 feet square. Nick went to a local quarry (we live on the edge of the Canadian Shield in Ontario, so limestone and granite abound) and selected 25 massive rocks to set in the garden. The boulders were transported by truck, and the men used the backhoe to arrange the boulders in a sweeping semicircle around the dug out slope. Three large, flat rocks formed the steps down into the garden. The south end remained open to the field and woods.

Nick's vision was to use the rocks and pea stone as the main focus of the space. He leveled the ground, laid landscape fabric and brought in a truck-

26

load of pea stone which he raked into an arc in the center of the garden. Between the rock wall and the pea stone floor he left a space about one yard deep that would be for plants. He set a large, high, flat stone opposite the rock wall. The area is about 420 square feet. Hans searched our land for granite slabs to house the urn. He found just the right ones and built a niche into the wall, just off center, under a big, overhanging Ponderosa pine. I dug the flower beds. The result was a Japanese flavor, sunken, meditative garden!

Since we weren't absolutely confident about just going to the cemetery and digging up the urn without talking to the minister who conducted Rachel's funeral, we invited the minister and his family over for coffee and told them about our plan. We received their full support. As soon as they left, Hans and Nick threw some topsoil into Nick's pickup, drove down to the cemetery, dug up the urn, filled the hole, brought Rachel "home" and placed her in her niche in her garden. The relief I felt to have Rachel's ashes near is indescribable. A neighbor who is a potter had made Rachel's urn, and the ferrier for her horse Half-Pint made the iron clasp. Half-Pint's winter shoes are in the niche too.

A GARDEN FOR RACHEL

It was now October, but the weather still held. October 14 is Rachel's birthday. I knew that the only way to get through that day was to have a birthday party for her, as we normally would have done. We invited our friends and neighbors to come for coffee and birthday cake, and to bring a plant for Rachel's garden, from their own garden, as a birthday gift for Rachel. Japanese and Siberian iris, bleeding heart, lavender, campanula, goose neck loosestrife, ajuga, lamb's ears, white phlox, pink perfection lilies, various sedums, a Golden Globe Cedar shrub and three Colorado Blue Spruce arrived. All were dormant but with the promise of the coming spring. A friend who is a wood carver brought a piece of cherry wood with Rachel's name and dates and a little sleeping angel carved on it. We hung it on the Ponderosa pine.

Another friend who makes arbors, trellises and baskets brought an arbor made out of split cedar rail. Friends gave an alder twig love seat for the garden.

Since that October, I have planted some small daylilies: Little Sweetie, Dancing Shiva and Stella d'Oro. I have planted a William Baffin Explorer climbing rose on the arbor and have added a peony, delphinium and monarda to the beds. In the summer I tuck white Sweet Allysum and Dusty Miller in around the perennials. Blue Carpet Juniper and creeping phlox grow in the spaces around the rocks on the upper level. Next year I want to plant Flower Carpet ground cover rose in the smaller of the two openings on the south side of the garden. I also want to add some ornamental grasses. I have also found a daylily called "Rachel, My Love."

You can get to the garden from the driveway without coming up to the house. Just walk through the arbor, along the pea stone path. I sometimes find that flowers and notes have been left for Rachel. I once found a ribbon there tied to the tree. You can also approach the garden from further up the driveway. Just step into the sumac, say "hello" to St. Francis as you pass him, take a few steps along a flagstone path, down a few rock steps, and you are in another world, it seems. In the spring this path is covered with yellow daffodils and blue scilla.

It is a different garden in the winter. Although inaccessible it is beautiful as the snow drifts up against the rocks and around Rachel's niche, now stuffed with pine boughs to keep her warm and protected. Each Christmas Hans strings colored lights through the pine tree. We can see the reflection, soft and pretty on the snow at night. There is a permanent lamp attached to the branches of the Ponderosa pine above Rachel's cherry wood memorial plaque. The light comes on automatically at dusk.

Hans and our friends say that Rachel is there in the garden: in the tree, around the land, on the road, at the little school she loved, with her horse, and in all our hearts.

Chapter 5
Katie's Garden: An Alcoa, Tennessee, School's Tribute

School teacher Silvia Roca came home from Katie Deal's funeral wondering again how she could help her little second-graders cope with the death of their classmate. Because Alcoa Elementary is a multi-grade school, Silvia had moved up with her class each year, teaching them from kindergarten through second grade. The children had been together for three years, and Katie's battle with cancer had been a part of those years. The little girl's family described Mrs. Roca as Katie's "favorite person in the world," and Silvia had visited Katie at home before her death. She had to come up with a special way to manage her own sorrow as well as the children's.

Silvia recalls: "I wanted to do more than plant a tree, so my children and I decided to plant a butterfly garden."

First, to begin fundraising for the garden, the students suggested making a sign to announce the garden to the other classes. The sign, displayed in the school library, said "Katie's Garden" and was liberally illustrated with the children's drawings. Some drew hats recalling the ones Katie wore during chemotherapy. Others drew hands with brightly painted fingernails like Katie's. Others wrote personal messages like "I love you, Katie."

Next, the students began to plan their garden by compiling a three-page wish list including a deck, covered bench, bird bath, butterfly houses, paths, and a long, detailed list of flowers. The garden would be bright and happy just like Katie. Her favorite colors — pink, red, white, and yellow — would attract the butterflies that she had loved to chase. One kindergartner at the school said the garden would be "a place where angels play."

Donations of money, materials, and skills came from parents, local businesses, garden clubs, and the city government. Students made sacrifices for the project, such as donating their ice cream money. Each class contributed something for the garden — trees, bulbs, fountain, statuary, butterfly houses and stepping stones. Silvia says, "Our original plans were to spend about $500, and things 'blossomed' into a $5000 garden."

Participation was widespread. Since it was January when the project began, the children started seeds for many of the plants indoors. Every student in the school planted at least one seed. Adult volunteers constructed the deck, fence, and walkways, but much of the digging and planting was done by the children themselves. On a visit to the garden, our third-grader guide announced imperiously, "I built this garden myself. Well, somebody else built the fence, but I painted it."

The shape of the garden is a free-form one that was predetermined by the space available in front of the school. It surrounds a raised octagonal deck, which is large enough to accommodate a class of children. In front of the deck is a small brass sign that says "Katie's Garden." The seats on the deck are a comfortable height for elementary students, though not too small for adults.

The paths in the garden are made of molded, white concrete "stones." Since children are fond of stepping stones, this design helps to keep them from trampling flower beds. The paths take you from one gate to the other, across the deck or around it, and into some alcoves within the garden.

A white picket fence with a scalloped top surrounds the garden. The fence has two gates so that you can enter the garden at one end, walk through, and exit on the other side, but the path is winding enough that it discourages use of the garden as a convenient shortcut. The fence is low enough to let people see and enjoy the garden without necessarily going inside it every time.

The scale of the garden is primarily for children. The child-sized, covered bench provides a cozy spot of shade in the bright garden. The statuary, birdbaths, and fountain are small enough that they don't overshadow young visitors. The redbud, pink dogwood, and other trees will grow larger than they are now but were selected so that they will remain a child-friendly scale, never towering over the garden.

The variety in Katie's Garden is tremendous. Salvia, dianthus, pansies, marigolds, gerbera daisies, geraniums, columbine, creeping phlox, azaleas, red honeysuckle, irises, shasta daisies, and butterfly bush are only some of the many kinds of flowers that the children at Alcoa Elementary can learn about.

The many ornaments are almost a treasure hunt for the young visitor. At the gate near Silvia's classroom there is a suggestion box, a white mailbox brightly decorated by one of the students. Ahead toward the right is a little statue of an angel with a cluster of forget-me-nots planted in front of it. Next to it are three blue metal butterflies, only slightly larger than life-size, and a tiny plastic bird with movable wings entertains the most observant visitor.

Water in the small pool circulates through the top of a statue of two young children standing under an umbrella. There is a traditional birdbath made of concrete and another made by stacking brightly painted terra cotta pots topped by a terra cotta saucer. Two butterfly houses and a tile mosaic butterfly in the path reinforce the butterfly theme. The most touching ornament of the garden is one that may be overlooked by the casual observer. On the pathway just inside each of the two gates, there is an imprint of Katie's tennis shoes and her initials, K.D.

Silvia realized that vandalism can be a problem with many public gardens, so she encouraged a strong feeling of ownership among the community and the student body. The widespread involvement of so many people and the intensive publicity during all stages helped generate a proud and protective spirit among the many participants.

An estimated 900 people attended the dedication of Katie's Garden. Katie's family cut a ribbon at the entrance and sat on the deck. The students sat on a hillside overlooking the garden. Silvia spoke and thanked parents for putting up with their children coming home "filthy-dirty" every day while they were planting the garden. Students sang "Angels Among Us" and listened to an arrangement of "Friends." At the end of the dedication, they released butterflies into the garden.

The impact of the garden didn't end with its dedication. The deck serves as an outdoor classroom, and students continue to tend the flowers as a part of their education. Teacher Donna Redwine talks excitedly about the way her class watched monarch butterflies emerge in her classroom terrarium and then released them into the garden. When students visited a festival of trees at Christmas, they wanted to have one of their own in Katie's Garden. They obtained balled-and-burlapped trees that each class decorated, creating a pretty sight that the community turned out to see. Garden club members help students maintain Katie's Garden. This has given rise to a Junior Garden Club of 132 members and has been the site for at least one garden club flower show.

Katie's Garden succeeds in many ways. It is a comfortable place for children and adults. The bright, frisky colors and whimsical ornaments honor Katie's spirit. Most of all, Silvia says that the garden helped the healing process for Katie's classmates. The project, so notable for its involvement of large groups of people, is a source of pride for the school and community.

Chapter 6
The Becky Garden

In January 1995, I looked out the window at the ugly, messy patio. It was cluttered with a rotting tool shed, two half-barrels of weeds, a geodesic dome "playhouse," and a child-size picnic table. The cedar trees around the open patio had been broken by freezing rain 11 months earlier and the hollies were so overgrown that no one knew if the corner of the patio was rounded or square. Nothing had been done out there since Becky had gotten sick over a year before.

The only decent spot was "The Domino Garden," which 13-year-old Becky had asked for help in planting when Domino, our first dog, died. Pink and white begonias had flourished there for four summers, but this was January. All you could see of the garden now was the piece of tile on which Becky had painted "Domino 1973-1991." And now the Lewis family needed a Becky Garden, something pretty in memory of a sweet, beautiful girl.

I am the gardener in the family, but the chore of tearing down the shed and digging up the cedars and hollies was more than a one-woman job. The family pitched in, which provided a chance to work out some frustration together with vigorous, exhausting activity. Thirteen-year-old Jay was the first to say, "I just wish I could go outside and tear something up." We gave him a crowbar and the tool shed as a healthy outlet for his anger. My husband, Jim, does not care a bit for gardening, but the hollies were a good target for his frustrations. (We found that the corner of the patio was

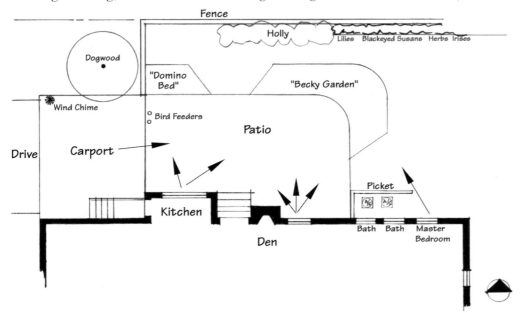

rounded.) I realized that when he felt unable to be demonstrative, he was still being supportive of me by participating in the work. Later, when seven-year-old Thomas was helping pick daffodils in the front yard for his sister's grave, he had a chance to express himself comparing her to a bud that was just opening: "She didn't have enough time, and then it was like winter came."

The plan for Becky's garden was simply to extend a bed about six feet from the edges of the patio across from the smaller Domino bed, leaving two openings to walk through to the yard. This placed Becky's garden where it would be visible from the carport, the kitchen, the den, and the master bedroom. With these vantage points, I can enjoy looking at the flowers when I sit at my sewing machine in the bedroom. We can also watch birdfeeders near the kitchen window during our meals. The pretty garden is the first thing to greet me when I drive into the carport and the last thing I see when I leave.

There is some irony in my choice of the color pink for the garden. I had always preferred yellow, regarding pink as sissy, and comparing it to a bottle of stomach medicine. All that changed when my baby girl was born, and the sweetness and delicacy of pink began to appeal to me. When Becky was old enough to have her own preferences, she chose to wear bright colors instead of pastels, but she had selected pink flowers for the Domino bed, and she would surely have indulged me in the decision to plant pink flowers for my "baby" girl's garden.

The color pink is what holds the garden together in spite of its wide assortment of plants. The project has been an experimental garden so far – where any flower that is pink (with some whites, purples, and blues) has been given an opportunity to show what it can do. To accommodate Becky's preference for bold colors, I made sure to include some deep pinks as well as light ones.

Until Becky's illness, I did not consider myself a sentimental person, but now in the garden I gave myself the license to let sentimentality run free. I bought several plants for the significance of their names. Becky was an exceptionally talented musician, so I planted coral bells and a "Bells" mix of snapdragons next to a small wrought-iron treble clef. I also found a white double petunia called "Sonata." "Fortissimo" daffodils and a "Blue Staccato" iris are in other areas of the yard where pink is not the rule. The little flower, Torenia, reseeds itself very well, and the assortment that I found was called "Clown Mix" — appropriate since Becky liked to wear a clown costume to masquerades.

Becky was sweet 16, the family's only girl. Now we would never see her walk down the aisle in my wedding dress that my mother made. This disappointed, never-to-be Mother of the Bride planted tulips named "First Kiss" and "Valentine," which also is my mother's maiden name. Peppermint gladioli called "My Love" performed well. Two of our pink daylilies are "Mother Like Daughter" and "Eternal." Other sentimental names included baby's breath, bleeding heart, and Cupid's dart.

One happy discovery was a variety of silver mound called "Angel Hair." Becky adored Angel, her blond cocker spaniel, and this plant is as fluffy and soft to touch as Angel's silky fur. I planted lycoris, which is sometimes called "Resurrection Lily", a symbol of hope. Becky would have snickered at another nickname for the lycoris: "Naked Ladies" (because of the way the flowers shoot up on tall stems with no surrounding foliage.)

Some of the plants were gifts and even heirloom plants. The music school had expressed sympathy by sending a pink azalea that found a place in the garden. My father gave me a start on some "Sweetheart" roses descended from cuttings that my music teacher had given him over 30 years ago. Memorial Easter lilies from the church have multiplied and bloomed in the Becky garden.

One gardening friend, Connie Scott, made several contributions, including dwarf hollyhock, evening primrose, and bee balm. I have been able to share baby hollyhocks with two neighbors who appreciate having plants that are associated with Becky's memory. Lamb's ear from Connie's yard brought back happy memories of a trip to the local botanical garden, where Becky and her two younger brothers were fascinated with the soft furry plant. Connie's Black-eyed Susans didn't go into the pink "Becky bed", but were a welcome addition in another part of the yard because it is the state flower of Maryland and represents where Jim and I spent our first three years of marriage.

A favorite family recollection of ours is when six-year-old Becky was playing tee-ball; she hit the ball and was on her way to first base when some nearby church bells began chiming. She slowed down, oblivious to everyone's voices shouting, "Run! Run!" After she was called out, she explained, "I wanted to hear the pretty bells." Those same church bells are audible in our yard, and I always stop to listen.

In addition to those distant bells, I wanted a wind chime. A jangling, discordant, high-pitched chime would never do in Becky's garden. Jim and I waited until we

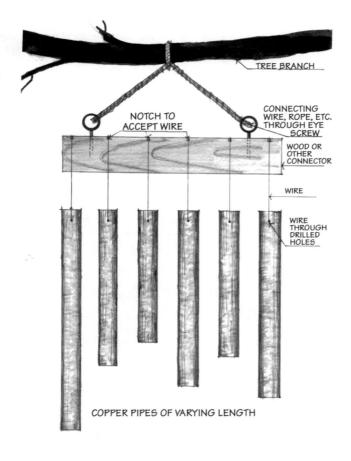

TREE BRANCH

NOTCH TO ACCEPT WIRE

CONNECTING WIRE, ROPE, ETC. THROUGH EYE SCREW

WOOD OR OTHER CONNECTOR

WIRE

WIRE THROUGH DRILLED HOLES

COPPER PIPES OF VARYING LENGTH

found a well-tuned (pentatonic), deep-voiced chime that provides a soothing sound. As welcome as the sound was, the big five-foot chimes looked entirely out of proportion to her small garden. I joked for a while about building a bell tower for them. However, I finally settled on their present location in the carport, where the large chimes are out of sight from the little garden, but well within hearing.

Although not every spot in the bed is always pretty, the "Let's try this" approach has provided enough variety that there is almost always something in bloom. Hardy mums reach their peak as the torenia turns brown and is discarded. Annual vinca gives way to the planting of tulip bulbs after the first hard frost. There is a constant ebb and flow from week to week.

In all, I have planted 30 to 40 varieties of plants in a fairly small area. Many of them have lived! When a salmon-pink clashes with a lavender-pink, I try to make a note to move them farther apart next year. Sometimes white flowers or plants that are not in bloom serve as a buffer between clashing shades.

Most gardens are a work in progress, and I expect to continue making changes every year. This year I will be dividing and sharing the white Becky daisies with more people, so that there will still be room in the garden for plenty of pink. In the years that follow, I may try to focus more on plants that have performed best, but there will always be new varieties to try.

Since my "apprenticeship" to Charles Sandifer while writing this book, I am doing more landscaping of the entire yard. But the area around the patio will always be a pink flower bed in memory of Becky.

Chapter 7
Charles' Garden Retreat

Many changes have taken place in this garden over the years. The miniature golf course that I built for the boys in one corner of the backyard is now a bed of daylilies. The highest point of the yard now includes a small deck, providing a vantage point of the whole garden.

Our overgrown lot behind our house has been cleared of briars, poison ivy, weeds, and undesirable saplings. We have converted this area, that we refer to as "the woods," into a neat wooded space with paths, foot bridges, plantings, a bench, and a hammock.

"We" included my son Richard, who died at the age of 30. Now the garden that he helped me build has become a place to mourn, a garden of memories — memories that tell a story. There is the "golf course" area where he and his brother Brian played golf. Beyond "the woods" I can see the open grassy area underneath the utility lines where I used to pass footballs and hit baseballs or play catch with Richard.

In the woods are two drainage ditches that, in a whimsical moment, Richard named "Fred and George" (I never did know for sure why he chose those names). There is the closed loop garden path that Richard helped me to lay out. We wheel-barrowed gravel in to cover and define the paths and make them more permanent. And there are the two oak trees with the hammock swung between them in which Richard loved to lie and read his beloved books.

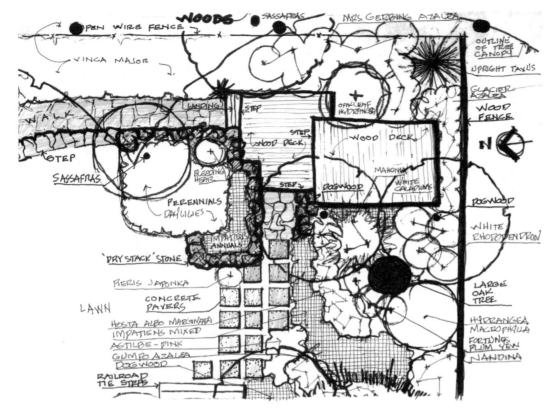

Labels on the plan (clockwise / as shown):

OPEN WIRE FENCE · WOODS · SASSAFRAS · MRS GERBING AZALEA · OUTLINE OF TREE CANOPY · UPRIGHT TAXUS · GLACIER AZALEA · WOOD FENCE · N · VINCA MAJOR · LANDING · STEP · OAKLEAF HYDRANGEA · WALK · STEP · WOOD DECK · WOOD DECK · DOGWOOD · STEP · BLEEDING HEART · SASSAFRAS · MAHONIA · WHITE CALADIUMS · DOGWOOD · PERENNIALS DAYLILIES · WHITE RHODODENDRON · 'DRY STACK' STONE · IMPATIENS ANNUALS · PERIS JAPONKA · CONCRETE PAVERS · LAWN · LARGE OAK TREE · HOSTA ALBO MARGINATA · IMPATIENS MIXED · ASTILBE - PINK · GUMPO AZALEA · DOGWOOD · HYDRANGEA MACROPHYLLA · FORTUNES PLUM YEW · NANDINA · RAILROAD TIE STEPS

I can see all of these places from the small deck that was meant to be a retreat from the world. It has now become a private place to grieve, to contemplate, and to remember.

In front of the deck I can look toward the right, past a curving bed of vinca major (periwinkle) to the yellows, reds, pinks, peach, and golds of the daylilies in the former miniature golf area. To the left from the deck I can see a mass of hostas, pachysandra and impatiens that provide many shades of Richard's favorite color, green.

The bright reds, pinks, fuchsia, salmon, white, and other colors found in the impatiens remind me of Richard's whimsical nature. I can just see his impish grin and hear his dry, witty comments as I view the sparkling colors against the backdrop of greens.

DECK

On the south side of the deck, I have privacy provided by a solid board on board fence, weathered to a soft gray. To the west is a grouping of mahonia and azaleas, and on the east there is a specimen oakleaf hydrangea. This light screening does not totally block my view of the house, enhancing a sense of seclusion, but not isolation. A large oak and two dogwood trees are also on the west side with branches arching over the deck to touch the sassafras limbs that reach up from the woods. In addition to providing shade, these trees serve the important function of forming a lower

overhead plane than the sky. The scale and proportion of this lower "ceiling" work better with the human figure, giving me a sense of being in a cozy, intimate space, a sheltering cocoon.

This pocket garden has served me well as a grief garden. I can allow my moments of sorrow and tears to occur with a great sense of privacy. When anger strikes me, the weeds and grass that need to be tamed are very near, and I can go pull and rampage with abandon. In less grief-stricken moments I have the views, vistas, and focal points to direct my vision to those areas and objects that invoke memories of happier times.

The garden is not finished. For that matter, it will probably never be completed, but will be treated as an ongoing project as I continue to add different elements that remind me of Richard. For example, he loved ships and airplanes and had always been fascinated by them. He had dreamed of attending the U.S. Naval Academy before he developed diabetes. Our home lies directly in the path of a landing pattern, and I never hear an airplane flying over without thinking of Richard.

So, one day I will place in some fashion the motif of his favorite ship (a sloop, the eighteenth-century sailing vessel that he called a "slope" early in his life) or an airplane in the garden. It may be in the gate or burned into the wood deck or as a statue or a fountain. Somewhere I'll put a gavel to commemorate the last years of his life when he was trying to work for a law firm and going to law school.

I'm sure other things will come to my mind as I sit thinking of Richard in the sanctuary of my own retreat.

A gate is a good place to add a commemorative element such as a ship, book, airplane, gavel, butterfly, or bird

Chapter 8
Kerry Zerr's Container Garden

People in Solana Beach, California, had seen Dr. Tony Armino bicycling to and from work many times during his 20 years of practice, but one morning in 1988, as Tony pedaled to work, he was killed by a drunk driver. Along with his wife and four children, one of the people most deeply affected by the tragedy was Kerry Zerr.

Kerry had been Dr. Armino's nurse for three years, seeing office patients with him every day. Besides being her employer, he was a cherished friend. Tony was so well known in the community that Kerry could never escape the reminders. At the grocery store, on the beach, or in church, former patients would identify her as Tony's nurse, begin talking about him and look to Kerry for support in their grief.

At the same time, she was often disappointed at the lack of support she received from others. She and Tony's wife remained very close during the first years when many acquaintances seemed incapable of sharing the grief that they felt. Everyone seemed to think that a few months should take care of the hurt.

One blow followed another. Kerry sought therapy for her grief, but the therapist had personal problems of his own. A few months into counseling, he committed suicide. Shortly after that, Kerry's grandfather died. Grief compounded by more grief pushed her into clinical depression. With the insight of a nurse, Kerry had herself hospitalized.

Even as a patient in the hospital, she couldn't escape the loss of Tony because the hospital staff was so caught up in it too. At some time during her stay, however, someone gave her a list of possible hobbies that included gardening. She had "dabbled" with gardening in college but had been absorbed in career and motherhood since then.

Kerry's first step into gardening was not particularly memorable. She thinks she went to a garden center and bought maybe an African violet for her house. Or it might have been a book she bought on gardening. As insignificant as that first step was, it was a turning point for Kerry. She likes to quote garden writer Allen Lacy as saying your life can be divided into two sections: Before Gardening and After Gardening.

Initially, she was "too immersed in grief to be conscious of the therapeutic benefit of gardening," but after a while she recognized that she had a gift for arranging the colors, textures, and forms of plants in an artistic way. Soon the eagerness to learn more and more took over, and she became an avid garden reader to develop her newfound skill.

Kerry says that a major benefit of gardening is that it helps a person "connect to life." It also helped her reconnect with the community. At the garden center, she found a new friend in its owner Evelyn Weidener. She made a "telephone friend" at Park Seeds in Greenwood, South Carolina. Casual greetings grew to friendships as she spent more time outdoors with her neighbors. By happy coincidence, even her new therapist was also a gardener, and some sessions included discussions of the qualities of different plants.

Although Kerry did not set out to do a memorial garden, Tony had been a gardener, so his presence was there. She recalls the mornings he would arrive at work with garden dirt still on his hands and she would send him off to scrub. She has planted carrots at her new house and remembers the way he used to take beta carotene supplements and devour his homegrown carrots until his complexion would turn orange.

Kerry once heard someone say that there is "a gift in every hurt and a hurt in every gift." Gardening was certainly the gift that grew out of her hurt. One year she designed a hanging basket for a contest sponsored by Thompson & Morgan seed company, winning the grand prize — $100 worth of seeds yearly for the rest of her life. She has even changed careers from nursing to design and sales at a nursery, and one of her hanging baskets was featured in the June 1997 issue of *Sunset* magazine.

The first time Catherine spoke with her was a few days before Mother's Day, one of the busiest for the flower business. Kerry wasn't quite sure that day whether her new vocation was any less stressful than the old one!

Kerry says that one of gardening's valuable lessons is that grief, like gardening, is a process and not an end product. Grief changes in character from week to week just as a garden does, and you come back again and again to work on it. She says, "One of the wonderful things about a garden is that there is always renewal there, and what a blessing."

Chapter 9
Container Gardens

Today Kerry has a 100' x150' yard where she is developing flower borders, a shade garden, and a vegetable garden with plenty of carrots, but her gardening began on an 8' x 15' condominium terrace. The lack of a large piece of land does not prevent the development of a beautiful garden. Through experimentation, Kerry came up with some valuable principles for container gardening in a small space.

At first she planted whatever looked pretty to her, but she found that this began to look haphazard and messy in a confined area. To give a better sense of coherence, she now recommends using uniform containers. She uses only terra cotta pots or synthetic ones that look like terra cotta. This avoids a cluttered, disjointed look and calls more attention to the plants themselves. On her terrace she achieved further unity by sticking to a limited color palette of blues, pinks, lilacs, and a little white, although she did yield to the temptation to introduce a bright accent at times.

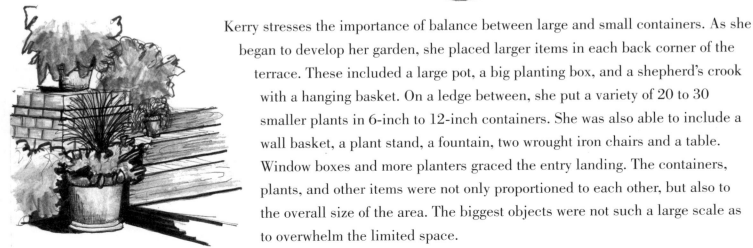

Kerry stresses the importance of balance between large and small containers. As she began to develop her garden, she placed larger items in each back corner of the terrace. These included a large pot, a big planting box, and a shepherd's crook with a hanging basket. On a ledge between, she put a variety of 20 to 30 smaller plants in 6-inch to 12-inch containers. She was also able to include a wall basket, a plant stand, a fountain, two wrought iron chairs and a table. Window boxes and more planters graced the entry landing. The containers, plants, and other items were not only proportioned to each other, but also to the overall size of the area. The biggest objects were not such a large scale as to overwhelm the limited space.

The light on Kerry's terrace was filtered shade in the morning and more shade in the afternoon. In the winter the shade was dense, so she moved those plants needing the most sun from the terrace to a sunnier landing. (This is one of the advantages to a container garden, where plants are portable enough to follow the changing patterns of sunshine or to bring inside when the temperatures drop.)

A terrace like Kerry's really does become an outdoor room, and as such, it needs housekeeping to remain tidy. She had to learn to allow herself to throw things away. A small space won't support too many ailing plants before the whole area begins to look ramshackle, so a sick plant that will recover only after months of ugliness should probably just be replaced. Good gardeners learn the valuable lesson that you can't fix everything.

As Kerry became more selective in her choice of plants, she found that it helped to consider the effect of each plant on the whole project. She had a hydrangea that displayed beautiful blooms but only for a short period of time. The rest of the year, it detracted from the looks of the terrace, so she donated it to the commons area of the condominiums, where it was more useful.

You can only bend the rules of nature so far, so remember that some plants will not fit your site, no matter how much you love them. Two plants that Kerry "bent over backwards" to grow were morning glories and cornflowers, but there was not enough sun in her garden for them. Rather than continue trying to fit a square peg into a round hole, she took pleasure in the plants that did thrive there. *Dipladenia rosea*, a vine commonly called Mandevilla, produced beautiful pink flowers. She had two pots of zephyr lilies, which are like small pink amaryllis, that enjoy a little crowding in a pot, tolerate rain and drought, and have grassy leaves that arch nicely. Nemisia, stock, linaria, fuschia, cyclamen, primrose, and begonia also thrived.

In addition to the flowering plants, variegated foliage brightens shady corners. Kerry likes plants with variegated foliage, such as variegated mint and variegated vinca. Kerry enjoyed her wall basket of *Glechoma* (ground ivy), that she placed at eye level. In about eight weeks, it grew long enough to cascade gracefully to the ground.

Container gardening doesn't always mean only one plant per pot —containers with a combination of plants often please the eye. When Kerry plants combination containers, as a general rule of thumb, she recommends putting something tall at the back and something "roundy-moundy" in the middle. Trailing plants tucked around the edges of the planter complete the design and soften the edges. Set plants close together in the pot using a light, enriched potting mix that includes peat and vermiculite. Ever since the time she planted one window box with regular fertilizer and the other with a slow release one, Kerry has recommended the slow release.

For hanging planters she prefers natural looking moss baskets over any kind of pot. They need to be watered once or even twice a day, but it is virtually impossible to over water them. Kerry likes to keep variegated perennials in the baskets as an anchor to the design, putting in some annuals each year for color. Unlike a pot, the basket allows you to plant through the sides as well as across the top. Kerry's baskets are "living balls of color" by the end of the season.

The availability of lightweight planting mixtures makes it possible to garden in containers even on balconies or rooftops. Find out where supporting beams are for placing heavier plants. Consider the downstairs neighbors and check drainage. Don't limit yourself to standard bedding plants, but include climbing or trailing vines that provide lush foliage without requiring a lot of root space.

The disadvantage to container gardening is that plants in containers are less forgiving of neglect than those planted in the ground. With regular care, however, a container garden offers the

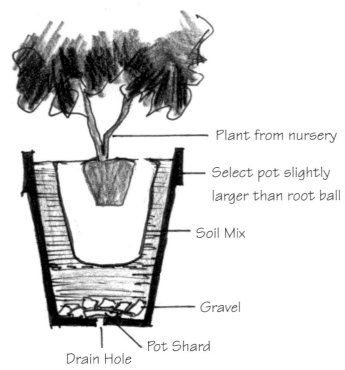

Plant from nursery

Select pot slightly larger than root ball

Soil Mix

Gravel

Pot Shard

Drain Hole

When repotting a plant, choose a pot that is slightly larger than the original. If roots have become bound into a tight mass, you may need to gently separate them so they will grow into the surrounding soil.

44

advantages of versatility and mobility. As plants go in and out of their prime, you can rearrange your garden with ease to showcase whatever appeals to you the most at any given time.

Container gardening encourages a higher level of intimacy with your plants as you nurture each individual one. Even if you have a large in-ground garden, keep some container plants for year-round pleasure indoors.

Chapter 10
Butterfly Gardens

Butterflies are such wonderful, living illustrations of resurrection. Although we may not see it, we know that the life cycle of the butterfly begins when a tiny caterpillar hatches from an egg. A few varieties of caterpillars may be considered attractive in a way, but many are unsightly and very destructive as they devour leaves. They grow hundreds of times their original size before finally wrapping themselves in cocoons where they appear to be dead. The cocoon or chrysalis hangs for about two weeks and then begins to tremble with life. After a struggle of several hours, the transformed caterpillar emerges as an adult butterfly with the ability to fly to places that the caterpillar never dreamed possible.

Butterfly gardens make excellent memory gardens. Another school butterfly garden is at Oglethorpe Point Elementary School, St. Simon's Island, Georgia. The garden was already under construction as an outdoor classroom when little Sutton Walker Jones drowned. Members of the community were touched and dedicated the garden in his memory.

This garden is in a sunny, rectangular-shaped area next to the school building. In each of the back corners are two butterfly bushes *(Buddleia davidii)*. Next to each pair of butterfly bushes are about eight sunflowers. An arc of azalea bushes is filled in with impatiens and other bright flowers.

The children go through the garden on square stepping stones and use round stepping stones to walk among the flowers for a closer look. Host plants for the caterpillars include parsley, dill, cabbage, and carrots. In addition to the brightly colored flowers for nectar, the garden has two fruit buckets, and a shallow plastic tub recessed into the ground to gather rain water.

The memorial plaque in the garden reads, "A butterfly lights beside us like a sunbeam. And for a brief moment its glory and beauty belong to our world. But then it flies on again, and though we wish it could have stayed, we feel so lucky to have seen it."

To attract butterflies to your garden, you need six things:

Sun

Butterflies are cold-blooded insects. Therefore, their body temperature changes with their surroundings. Their bodies must achieve a temperature of 85 to 100 degrees in order for them to be active and fly. So if the air is cool they have to sun themselves. Provide some stone surfaces (path, wall, edging, etc.) that will reflect the sun's heat for butterfly basking.

Food for caterpillars

Caterpillars are voracious eaters, and the adult butterfly will lay her eggs on a source of caterpillar food. Different varieties of caterpillars prefer different "host plants." See Chart 10.1 at the end of this chapter for a sampling. You cannot overestimate how much hungry caterpillars will eat, and they will leave a host plant looking tattered, so plant these in a less conspicuous part of your garden.

Food for adult butterflies

These are the pretty flowers that you will enjoy displaying in your garden. They provide nectar, which is the primary source of nutrition for adult butterflies. In general, select brightly colored flowers that have easy-to-reach centers and a flat surface for resting. Although you may find it distasteful, butterflies also love it when you provide overripe fruit for them. You may want to place this fruit on basking stones or use commercial feeders.

Shelter

Butterflies need a retreat from wind, rain, and predators. Fancy butterfly houses are attractive but not necessary if you have trees, shrubs, some uncut grass, or a wood or brush pile.

Moisture

Water is available to butterflies from the plants and from sources you provide, such as birdbaths, ponds, and mud puddles. Male butterflies drink from mud puddles, a habit called "puddling." This gives them extra sodium and amino acids that they pass along to the females to help them produce eggs. Allow your garden hose to leak very slowly on a bare patch of earth, and watch for visits from these butterfly fellows.

Absence (or minimum use) of pesticides

What needs to be said? Butterflies are insects; insecticides kill insects. At least avoid broad use of insecticides. If you see a specific problem area, such as an aphid attack on one section of irises, check around for beneficial insects like ladybugs, which eat aphids. If you find none, then choose a windless day to spray only the affected area, never your entire garden.

Many memory gardens have used the image of the butterfly. For Nora's Garden at Lausanne Collegiate School in Memphis, students made concrete stepping stones. One student's stone reads: "What a caterpillar calls the end of the world is really the beginning."

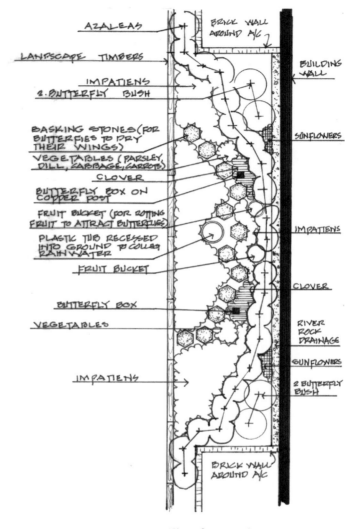

Plan for garden at
Oglethorpe Point
Elementary

Chart 10.1
Plants to attract butterflies

Host plants for caterpillars

Parsley*

Carrots*

Queen Anne's Lace*

Milkweed**

Aster

Bermuda grass

Clover

Hollyhock

Lupine

Mallow

Marigold

Passionflower

Plantain

Snapdragon

Sorrel

Violet

Fennel

* Preferred by swallowtails.

** Required by monarchs.

Nectar plants for adult butterflies

Asters and daisy-formed flowers

Joe-Pye weed

Vinca

Lantana

Liatris

Butterfly weed

Pentas

Coreopsis

Salvia

Phlox

Yarrow

Calendula

Cosmos

Bee balm

Impatiens

Nasturtium

Zinnia

Petunia

Chapter 11
Designing Gardens

Because of the emotional nature of a memory garden, we have not yet discussed the usual rules for designing a garden. Initially, the most important thing is to get outdoors and make a start, any start, on your garden, hopefully inspired by the examples we have given you. We didn't want you stymied, staring at a blank piece of graph paper. Now after getting the basics in place, you may feel like most other gardeners who like to take time to sit back, savor the results, and begin to dream of improvements.

Think about the types of gardens you prefer as your own philosophy of gardening emerges. There are some elements that will help you define what you want your garden to be, but always think of these as helps, not dictates.

First, ponder these physical considerations of your site: size, topography, views, orientation, circulation, screening and change.

Size

Many gardeners are lured by beautiful pictures in magazines and catalogs during the comfortable days of spring, and they forget that the work of gardening continues through the hot summer and beyond. If you decide you are ready to expand on the small start you made, think of the availability of both space and work force. Plan to use only a fraction of what is available.

A 100 square foot (10'x10') "pocket garden" can include specimens of most things you want to grow. Most individuals can maintain an area of about 900 square feet (30'x30'), and many garden enthusiasts enjoy still bigger spaces. Enlarge it a little at a time, season by season, as you determine the amount of help you will get and the measure of your own time, energy, and interest.

Topography

The term "topography" means the permanent features of your property: the lay of the land and things like buildings, trees or large shrubs that are not going anywhere. Is your site hilly or flat? You may decide to change

the contour of the land by filling in low places, creating small hills ("berms"), or making raised beds. You could also choose to work around the existing topography, such as using a low area for a bog garden. Many times people tame a steep hill, not by removing it, but by terracing it. This provides level areas for planting and steps that give you a better walking surface.

Your resources will influence what you decide to do with your topography. Marian Sinn knew someone who had a backhoe, which was used to carve out a hillside for Rachel's Garden. The people at Alcoa Elementary designed Katie's Garden to fit the space already determined by the layout of sidewalks in front of the school. An awareness of the topography can help you decide how to change your site or plan a garden that works with it.

Views

When you stand in a particular area of your garden, what do you see? Do you see a flowering shrub or your air conditioning unit? As you look beyond your property line, do you see your neighbor's beautiful garden or his compost pile? As you move from point to point in your garden, you have many views in every direction. You can control the views by where you place things (orientation) or how you hide them (screening).

You may want to establish a focal point for your garden, a strong visual element that attracts you. More often than not, a focal point is a man-made object: a statue, fountain, or seating area, but it could be a particularly striking specimen plant. If you want a really strong pull toward the focal point, consider something like a straight path toward it. This type of feature, called an "axis," may be stronger than you want, or you could make our example even stronger by bordering the path with a hedge. An axis can be useful, not only in attracting attention to a focal point, but also in drawing attention away from less desirable views.

Orientation

Orientation refers to positioning of the garden in relation to the rest of your property. When Catherine originally planted the Becky Garden around her patio, Charles had not yet explained orientation to her. It was dumb luck that the garden is visible from the carport, the backyard, and three rooms of the house; or it was the good design sense of the person who first built the patio. We say this to stress again that, while knowledge will help, you shouldn't let the lack of knowledge keep you from starting a garden.

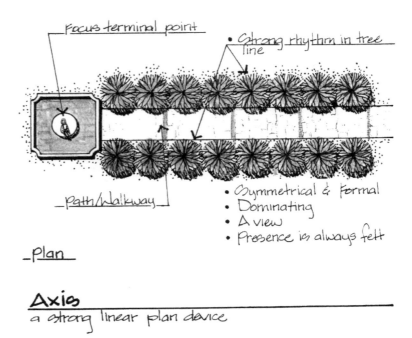

Focus terminal point

Strong rhythm in tree line

Path/Walkway

- Symmetrical & Formal
- Dominating
- A view
- Presence is always felt

Plan

Axis
a strong linear plan device

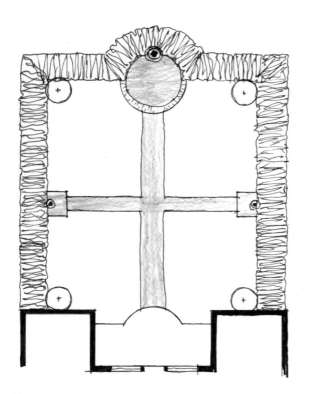

Good orientation is convenience. Whether you plant your garden north, south, east, or west of your house, you can find plants specific for any of these locations. The more important point is whether you can see the garden easily and walk there conveniently.

Circulation

Once you get to the garden, can you move around easily within it? If it is large enough to have a path, can you get out as easily as you can get in? As the illustrations show, a path can take you to a distant point and back the same way, or with more available space it can loop around and bring you out near the place you began. A curving path slows you down more than a straight, "bee-line" path. Since a memory garden is for contemplation, we favor the slower, curved path.

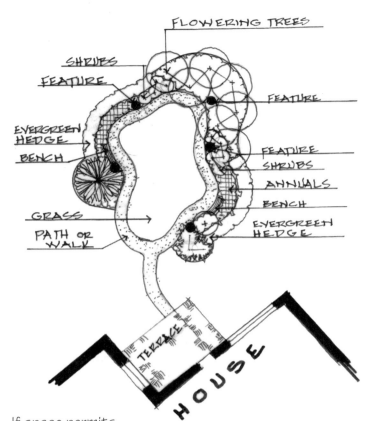

If space permits,
a loop path can guide the visitor through a relaxing route with many points of interest along the way

If you are designing your own path, try one of the easier, more temporary construction techniques until you are sure it's the route you want. You could start with stepping stones or use mulch that can be turned under if you change your mind. Once you are sure, you may want to convert to a permanent material like concrete or brick. Don't underestimate the width you need for the path. To push your wheelbarrow down the path, you will need about three feet. To walk side-by-side with a companion, you'll need four to five feet.

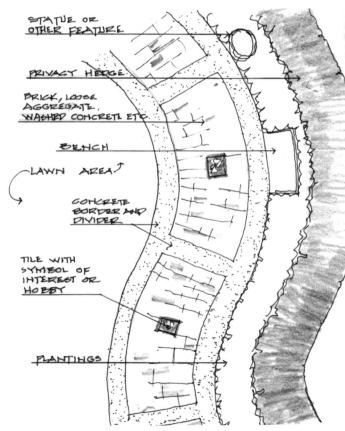

The sale of engraved bricks can help raise funds for a public garden, or you may want to use some in your own private garden.

A mixture of materials can add interest to a pathway. Here bricks are surrounded by concrete to give a variety of color and texture.

Screening

The decision about screening depends on the atmosphere you want for your garden. Do you want a visible, display garden? Would you rather have a high level of privacy? Or do you want something in between? You might get the best of both by letting your memory garden be an enclosed "garden room" within your larger property. Those good or bad views beyond your garden will influence your decision too.

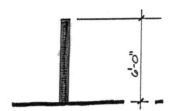

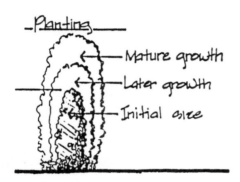

Screening can help to define the area that you've set aside for your memory garden. It doesn't have to be heavy or tall screening to establish the boundary of a special place. There are many possibilities for screening. Heavy screening, like a solid wall or fence, separates you from the sights and many sounds of the outside world. Lighter screening, such as a more open fence or a hedge, shields you from casual view but doesn't feel as isolated as a solid screen. A hedge is also a place for birds to find shelter. The birds' chirping and fluttering are natural sounds that help disguise outside noises like traffic or machinery. A lower hedge would allow you to see outside the garden when you are standing up but feel sequestered when you sit down.

Sometimes if the area is small, you could feel boxed in by too much screening. You can avoid feeling claustrophobic by opening one or more sides. You might also provide "windows" in the screening that reveal a pleasant view outside the immediate area.

Change

Nothing stays the same in a garden. The inevitability of change is one of the great life lessons we learn there, and it is also a practical challenge for every gardener.

You can predict a young plant's mature size to some degree by reading the seed packet, the catalog listing or the tag attached to the seedling at the nursery. Resist the temptation to plant a baby shrub within two feet of the house if the tag says that it will eventually have a spread of 10 feet.

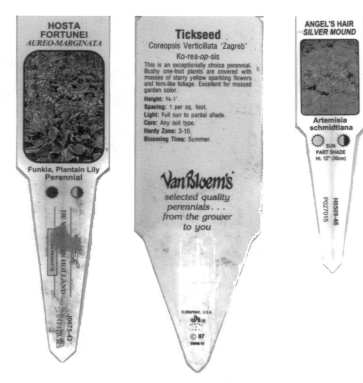

Plant tags can often supply a wealth of information about the plant you are buying. Catalogs are good sources as well, although their descriptions tend to be glowing in order to sell more plants.

Sometimes it is harder to find out how quickly a plant will reach its mature size, but this is an important factor. You know what you want for your garden, but how long are you willing to wait for it? You may want a fast-growing hedge for privacy, or you may be willing to wait for a slower plant that will require less frequent trimming. A knowledgeable person at the garden center can help you select the best plants for your needs.

In general, annuals grow much faster than perennials. Many annuals bloom steadily from spring, through summer, to the first frost or beyond. Perennials usually have shorter periods of bloom, but they make up for it by coming back on their own each year. Check the plant label for time of bloom. Select plants with different blooming times for a continual but changing show of color. Some species of perennials include early, midseason, and late varieties. By planting more than one variety, you can expect something, but not everything, to be in bloom at all times.

Light patterns change with the time of day and the seasons. The leaf patterns of deciduous trees (trees that drop their leaves in the fall) allow more sunlight to filter through in winter and less in summer. If the trees are trimmed high, they can let in more indirect light during morning and afternoon but block out the blistering heat of the noonday sun. Notice that areas to the north of your house may be in shadow in the winter but in full sunshine when the sun is higher in summer.

Just as a garden changes and grows, so do you. Your likes and dislikes, your physical ability to work in the garden, your schedule, maybe even your place of residence – all can change over time – but a garden is adaptable to all of these.

You can dig up a plant that didn't meet your expectations and replace it with something else. You can adjust garden size and contents to require less maintenance, or if you find more time, you can expand the project. If you have to move to another place, you will be able to take some, though not all, of your plants with you. As they take root and bloom and multiply, you will find satisfaction in the sense of continuity a garden can provide, even in the midst of change.

EVERGREEN   DECIDUOUS

Deciduous trees, such as oaks, maples, and elms, lose their leaves in autumn. Evergreens, like pine, fir and holly, keep their green leaves year round. Your garden has many uses for both kinds of plants.

Chapter 12
Gardening with an Artistic Eye

People's tastes are as individual as their fingerprints, but over the years, artists, designers, architects, and landscape architects have found some principles that apply to good design, no matter what the style. Some knowledge of these principles will help you understand why you like certain features better than others in your garden.

These principles are unity, balance, scale, proportion, rhythm, dominance, and accent.

Unity

Unity is a quality of oneness that pulls the design together expressing a single idea or purpose. It keeps your garden from being a hodgepodge, but it doesn't mean you can't have variety. The Becky garden is unified by the color pink, but it has 30 or more kinds of plants with different shades, heights, shapes, leaf textures, and flower types.

Repetition of any feature in your garden encourages a unified look. Kerry Zerr unifies an assortment of colors and sizes in a container garden by using only terra cotta colored pots. Katie's Garden is unified by the white color and curved lines of the fence and walkways.

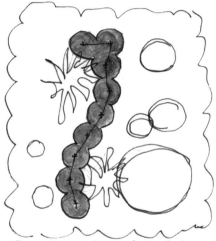

The connected line of small plants creates a sense of unity that a disjointed scattering of plants would lack.

A strong unbroken line of plant material (a hedge or low edging plant) or of manmade material (a walkway or retaining wall) can help an assortment of features look like they are meant to go together. Some people like to have several beds the same shape or to repeat a given shape in stepping stones, trellises or other structures.

Consistency in texture helps the unity of a garden too. A rustic garden, for example, will include rough textures like unfinished wood, coarse mulch, and gravel. If you keep unity in mind, you won't be tempted to buy an ornate, Italian Baroque lighting fixture for your Japanese garden.

Balance

In a balanced plan the whole composition appears in equilibrium. The simplest example is a formal garden, which uses symmetrical balance around a central point or line. Each side is a mirror image of the other. This bilateral symmetry may seem easier to design, but it is harder to maintain. The plants that were supposed to be twins often refuse to grow at the same rate and need constant pruning.

With asymmetrical balance, variations in size are less crucial. The result is usually a less formal, naturalistic garden. For this kind of balance, think of the visual weight on each side of the center. A tall plant on the left can be balanced by a cluster of medium height plants on the right.

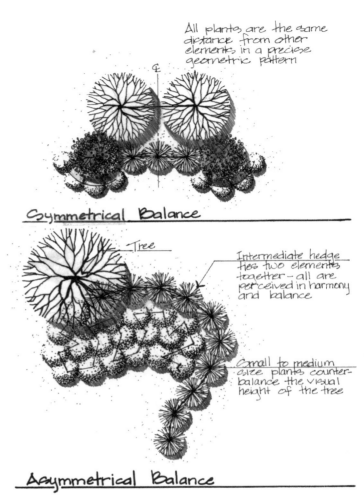

All plants are the same distance from other elements in a precise geometric pattern

Symmetrical Balance

Tree

Intermediate hedge ties two elements together – all are perceived in harmony and balance

Small to medium size plants counter-balance the visual height of the tree

Asymmetrical Balance

Symmetrical Balance

Asymmetrical Balance

Move things around before installing them to see how they balance each other. Some plants may not yet be their mature size, but you can add and remove plants to keep things balanced as they grow. If you can look at your garden without feeling the need to tilt your head or raise one shoulder, you're probably doing all right.

Scale

In design, scale is the size of an object in relation to the size of the person using the garden. Your perception of scale is basically determined by your eye level. The average height of eye level for most people standing up is four and a half to five and a half feet, less than that if you are sitting on a chair or bench, and still less if you are on the ground working in plant beds. You will want some things that require you to look up and some that make you look down.

A very large garden with big plants and a towering statue can be impressive and awe-inspiring, or it can make you feel intimidated, wishing for more comfortable, human-sized surroundings. A wide-open space can be divided into smaller ones the same way an interior designer divides a large room into smaller conversation groupings. An overwhelming single feature can be tamed down by balancing with a smaller grouping.

The scale of a garden influences how an individual feels and can be positive or negative .

Inside a small space, a person might feel cozy or claustrophobic.

A scale that accommodates the human size is usually the most comfortable.

In a large space, the person might feel insignificant or awed.

Personal gardens are more often small and intimate. While it might be possible to design a garden so small that you feel like Gulliver in Lilliput, this is not usually a problem. If your garden will be populated by children, get some miniature plants and accessories. A child-sized chair can make a nostalgic little plant stand when the children are grown.

Proportion

Another size relationship is proportion, the size of things in the garden compared to each other and compared to the whole. People sometimes select things for their gardens without thinking about the size of the great outdoors. When you shop for your garden, keep in mind that tiny plants you buy will grow, but an undersized planter or statue will only seem to get smaller as the living part of the garden grows around it.

If an object in your garden looks too insignificant or too imposing, you can adjust the proportion. Stu Upchurch kept his little cherub statue from looking lost on his terrace by surrounding it with blue and white flowers. The size of the space in Rachel's Garden is large enough that the surrounding boulders do not overpower it.

Rhythm

When elements in the garden are repeated at regular intervals, it sets up a feeling of rhythmic movement. The simplest

This small statue is out of proportion to the tree. The look could be improved by buying a larger statue or by moving the small statue farther away from the tree so that the statue isn't dwarfed by its towering neighbor.

example would be a row of trees, each one planted an equal distance from the next, marching into the distance in a precise cadence. This effect was put to good use by the Tulsa Kiwanis Club, which planted redbud trees along a stretch of highway as a memorial to victims of the Oklahoma City bombing. On a smaller scale you can use stepping stones, shrubs, or colorful plants at regular intervals to set up a gentle, harmonious cadence.

Rhythm can convey a sense of order without necessarily being formal. Most gardeners naturally avoid erratic repetition, which would be the opposite of rhythm. They are more likely to set up too strong a rhythm by taking two colors of flowers and alternating them along a row: red-white-red-white-red-white, for example. This unnatural arrangement of single plants would look softer arranged as repeating clusters of color. These clusters reflect the way things grow naturally when they reseed themselves near a parent plant, and they give the eye a chance to rest a little longer before going to the next color, providing a less driving rhythm.

60

Dominance

Dominance is the use of one outstanding element to which all else is subordinate. To many people this means a focal point, such as a gazebo or fountain or the view of a mountain or lake. In a memory garden, the focal point may be a statue. Most of us could not afford an expensive, custom-made sculpture of the actual person honored in the garden, but there are many ready-made statues available with characteristics that can remind you of your loved one. If you prefer a more indirect reminder, consider a focal point that suggests an interest or a hobby. It might be a concrete animal, a wrought-iron ship, or anything else that appeals to you.

A single focal point is not the only way to establish dominance. It could also mean a flower bed planted with a single color or a motif that is repeated in several of the garden beds throughout the project. As someone looks at the garden, he recalls having seen this same design pattern in another part of the garden. Use of a single dominant factor in the garden gives great visual impact and can help the sense of unity. This simplifies the garden by providing a single trait that is easily recognized as the most important.

Accent

Similar to spice or salt in food, accent is the counterpoint, the thing that makes the dominant clearer. It is the difference between two objects that sets up a pleasant tension or contrast. If the dominant factor is a color, such as red, then it might be surrounded by white to contrast with it and make it show off more. A small accent breaks up monotony without being disruptive.

A small shrub with a round form contrasted with tall larger shrubs adds accent

Many people like to inject a touch of whimsy into their gardens, even in a memory garden. Consider placing something in the garden that your loved one would find amusing or ironic. It may also be the little lift your spirit longs for.

A tall shrub among a bed of low spreading plants also adds accent

A potted geranium on the table on the terrace can add accent

Chapter 13
Design Tools

Whatever effects you want to create in your garden, you use a combination of four basic design tools (called structural elements of art) to accomplish them. Remember that your garden is three-dimensional, so you will use these design tools in several different planes.

The first area most gardeners think about is the base plane, the ground or "floor." This is where you lay out the beds, paths, lawn, and other "flat" designs. If you have sketched a plan on paper, you have drawn the base plane.

When you place tall plants behind shorter ones, consider screening, or add something upright like a tree or trellis, you've begun to think of vertical planes. Vertical planes form the "walls" of your garden, as well as anything within these walls that makes your eye look up and down.

Probably the last plane you have considered, but an important one, is the overhead plane. Do the trees in your yard form a natural "ceiling" in part of your garden? Do you want to lower the overhead plane in one area by building an arbor or a pergola? Or will the sky literally be the limit as you gaze heavenward from your sunny garden?

The four structural elements of art – line, form, texture, and color – will be useful in all three of these planes. You can combine these four to set a mood and even create optical illusions.

Line

Look around and you will discover that all elements of a garden have line quality. Lines can go in every direction in every plane. The edges of your beds form lines in the base plane. The top of the hedge forms a horizontal line through the vertical plane. The tree provides a vertical line in the vertical plane. Lines can be straight or curved, smooth or rough, strong or weak. They can evoke different emotions (see Chart 13.1).

A man-made shelter like this pergola can create an area with a cozy, low overhead plane.

In general, it's best not to mix many radically different kinds of lines. If you have one flowerbed with curved lines, it could be jarring to plant a square bed nearby. Of course, this doesn't mean you never mix line types. If your house has very straight lines and classical design features, you might choose to continue those lines in a formal looking garden, or you might want to soften the look by rounding out the sharp corners with soft, curved plantings.

If you want to call attention to a particular feature, you might introduce a different kind of line, but this can be a very strong technique. A straight path through a garden of curved lines may command you to move directly to a focal point and not dilly-dally along the way, while a curved path would coax you more gradually to the focal point. A circle in the middle of a straight-lined garden will place a sense of importance in the round space. It is still consistent with the straight lines, however, because the circle is a geometric shape and not just a freeform blob in the middle of a formal garden.

Horizontal

Vertical/Upward

Chart 13.1

Lines and Emotions

Upward/Vertical - noble, inspirational, aspiring, going up in life, moving closer to God

Parallel - sense of harmony, peace

Horizontal - calming, one in harmony with earth

Non-rigid - fluid, soft, reflects nature, peaceful, calming

Erratic - confusing, chaotic, lack of order, stressful

Intersecting - confusing, opposing, requiring a choice

Jagged - brutal, disconcerting, threatening, excitable, nervous, jittery

A few smooth, strong lines will be less confusing than many weak ones. For example, a single path that follows a flowing, unbroken route will be more relaxing than multiple short paths that shoot out in many directions. Sometimes a physical line has to be broken but can continue as an imaginary line. You may need an opening to walk through a hedge, but if the top of the hedge on both sides of the opening is the same height, your eye will move across that opening as if the line were unbroken.

Lines give you a chance to play with optical illusions. Imagine looking down a straight highway. The edges of the highway seem to converge in the distance at a point, a "vanishing point." Design a path so that it actually does get narrower toward the back of the garden, and those converging lines will make the garden look deeper. If your garden is actually too deep, you can open the space by making the path a little wider in the distance so that it looks shorter.

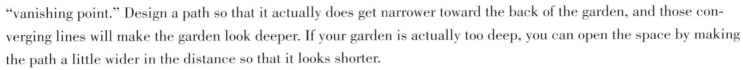

Form

The mention of form may conjure up images of shrubs meticulously trimmed into perfect spheres or cones, but simply stated, form means shape. It is not only the shape of an object but also the shape of an empty space. These shapes can be two-dimensional like the form of the terrace on the base plane, or three-dimensional like the form of a plant or an accessory. They can be familiar geometric shapes or free forms made with curved lines.

One classic use of forced form is the topiary, that careful trimming of shrubs to create special designs. Many gardeners, inspired by big, leafy sculptures of Mickey Mouse at Disney World, have returned home to try their hand at this technique. For most, it is a passing whim that eventually proves too time-consuming for the amateur gardener. A shortcut to the effect of topiary is to construct a shape out of wire mesh and allow a vine to cover it.

PYRAMIDAL

ROUNDED

SPREADING

COLUMNAR

The garden device called parterre is another way that people have empha-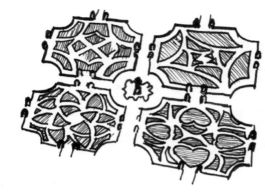
sized form. These usually formal gardens consist of shaped beds separated
by paths and forming a geometric design. At The Greenfield Village in
Dearborn, Michigan, Mrs. Henry Ford helped design a small parterre
garden in front of the Martha and Mary Chapel in honor of Mr. and Mrs.
Ford's mothers. The shapes, if pushed together, are meant to form a perfect
circle.

An awareness of forms doesn't necessarily lead to a formal design. Many
plants can be selected for the shapes they naturally assume, making it
unnecessary to force a shape with pruning shears. You'll also want to
mix some forms so that the garden doesn't get boring. As with lines, a
few large forms are better than many smaller ones. For example, if you
have two trees close enough together, you might plant one large, connecting bed that includes both. This would be more attractive than two
small, unconnected beds – and a lot less headache to mow around.

Forms also reflect certain traits (see Chart 13.2). In a memory garden, a weeping form can take on particular significance. The weeping willow has been a symbol for mourning in poetry and song. It is a large tree with a broad canopy
and prefers moist soil. You may want to use a weeping form in a smaller size, such as weeping yaupon holly or a
trailing vine.

Even small children have a sense of form in design. When Becky was a little girl, Catherine allowed her to cut away
low branches in the back of a china fir tree (*Cunninghamia lanceolata*) to create a hideout. The shape of the space she
carved was a nice, symmetrical arch. Sometimes adults need a hideout too. If you have a low-branching tree or a very
large shrub, you may be able to remove a few branches to create a similar retreat.

Chart 13.2

Forms and Traits

Cube – Not a natural plant form but a very stable form for objects like benches, tables or raised beds. A garden surrounded by square walls would be a cube-shaped space, providing that "Secret Garden" feeling. Overuse of cube forms without any rounded forms to soften them would look harsh.

Cone/Pyramid – The most stable form, not something you would imagine tipping over. The tip points heavenward especially in taller versions. A natural shape that many plants assume with little or no pruning. Avoid inverted versions, which look unstable and are generally bad for the plant.

Sphere – A comfortable, "well-fed," satisfied shape. Circular objects, including round beds, encourage a feeling of completeness. Natural spheres are more accepted at this time than artificially created ones. The "meatball" shrub is out of fashion right now, except in extremely formal gardens.

Upright Cylinder – An uplifting form because it attracts the eye along a vertical line. Occurs naturally in some trees, such as lombardy poplars. The trunk of any tree that has been pruned high forms a cylinder. Manmade possibilities include columns or long wind chimes. Vines can be trained along a frame or post to create a vertical cylinder.

Horizontal – Parallels the line of the earth. Gives a sense of calm. There are many options for prostrate or creeping plant forms, from blue rug juniper to creeping phlox. A plan that included only horizontal forms would be boring. Punctuate them with some vertical accents.

Weeping – Traditionally associated with grief. Also induces contemplation. Gently waving branches are relaxing. Besides the familiar weeping willow, there are smaller shrubs such as weeping holly. Or create the effect with vines hanging from an overhead support. Water may flow from a fountain in a weeping form.

Arch – A very comfortable form because of its strength and sense of shelter. A canopy of trees can provide a natural arch. An arched arbor over a gate produces an inviting entry.

Free Form – Reminding you again that form is not always formal. Curved shapes, like those created by the meander of a stream, the slope of a valley or hill, are relaxing and natural. They set up a natural rhythm that is soothing and comfortable.

Texture

Texture in plants is provided mostly, but not entirely, by leaf size. Small leaves give us a fine texture; large leaves give us coarse texture. The leaves of grasses, shrubs and trees provide all the ranges in between. Leaf textures may be described as rough, smooth, granular, fibrous, coarse, medium or fine.

Texture is relative. For instance, a plant normally considered medium-textured, such as a nandina, may appear coarse-textured if it is used next to the fine-textured needle-like foliage of junipers. This same nandina could appear fine-textured if placed near the large, coarse leaf of the oak leaf hydrangea.

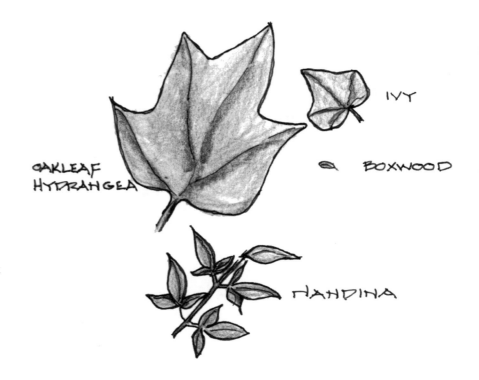

OAKLEAF HYDRANGEA

IVY

BOXWOOD

NANDINA

Plants have unlimited textural variations, and you can create any number of visual effects using different plants in conjunction with each other. The use of small-textured plants in the background can make that area seem farther away than it actually is because we expect distant objects to look smaller and less distinct. Large-leafed, coarse-textured plants in the background can make that same area seem closer.

The textures in the landscape are always changing. Spring textures will be different from fall textures, and those of the summer will be different from those of the winter. Textures can be found in the arrangement of the branching of plants and their twig formation; in the trunks, the roots and their leaves. Bark structure provides texture also. The birch tree is used in some areas specifically because of the bark texture. The exfoliating bark that is characteristic of the birch is continually peeling and seems to be reforming constantly, symbolizing rebirth and regeneration.

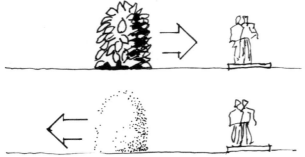

A coarsely textured plant will seem closer, while a finely textured plant will seem further away.

Beyond the visual effects, texture can provide tactile interest. Children and adults enjoy the fuzzy, velvety leaf of the lamb's ear. Silvermound is soft and fluffy and fun to touch. Cactus and English holly are a different story!

68

Color

Color has the most visual impact of any single factor. Emotional responses to color will be varied but strong. Sometimes it is just a matter of personal preference. One person may think a bronze-colored iris is elegant and sophisticated. The person standing next to him thinks the color looks muddy and tainted. Social customs also influence our response to colors. Fans of the TV series M*A*S*H will remember when Klinger presented a beautiful wedding gown to his Korean bride. She recoiled in horror and asked why he would want her to wear the color of mourning – white, according to Korean tradition.

Chart 13.3 outlines various colors and their emotional effects and physical characteristics. For most people, pastels and single-color combinations tend to be the most relaxing and calming.

Most people think of greens, blues, and purples as cool colors and yellows, reds, and oranges as warm ones. Dark tones are cool and relaxing, but can be depressing. Brights are considered "happy" colors that lift the spirit, but an overabundance of their giddy cheerfulness could be irritating in a grief garden. White flowers can glow with reflected light in a shady garden, as the sun sets, or even at night in the light of a full moon.

Dark colors seem to fade into the background, while light colors appear to come toward you.

Your decision about use of color begins with knowing whom the garden is for. You may want your own favorite color or that of the person the garden memorializes. If the garden is for children to use, like Katie's Garden, you will probably choose brighter colors than for an adult's contemplation garden.

When thinking about color, remember that flowers are not the only consideration. You have a wide range of colors available to you in the leaves of plants and even the stems. Manmade objects in your garden can contribute to your color scheme as well.

Use color in simple ways. If you want a natural landscape, plant colors in clusters as they would grow if the plants were seeding themselves. Blend one cluster into the next, just as naturally falling seeds would cross each other's boundaries.

Trust your instincts when you are drawn to a particular color. If a combination doesn't work out the way you wanted it to, you can change it next time or soften it by mixing in more white or green.

Chart 13.3

Color, Emotions and Physical Characteristics

Color	Emotional Effects	Physical Characteristics
Red	Exciting, vigorous, intense, striking. Can be aggressive or can represent love. "O, my Luve is like a red, red rose." (Robert Burns)	A little goes a long way. It is seen quickly so it attracts attention. Goes well with yellow and blue (completing a color triad). Complements green.
Orange	Festive, lively, encouraging, warm. Dynamic red mixed with energetic yellow.	A strong color like red. Goes well with kindred yellow and red. Complements blue.
Yellow	Energetic, cheerful, sunshine, warm. The color of young, spring leaves, new beginnings. Some grief gardeners may prefer a less perky, pastel yellow.	Almost every kind of flower has a yellow variety. Goes well with analogous oranges and reds. Complements purple. Completes a yellow-red-blue triad.
Green	Restful, cool, balanced, quiet. Suggests growth, fertility, life.	It is the center of the color spectrum. Harmonizes all other colors. Old-time engravers often kept a green gemstone nearby to look at when their eyes needed a rest.
Blue	Restful, serene, cool like water, calm like a sky in fair weather, heavenly, sincere ("true blue").	Most blue flowers seem to prefer cooler climates. May not always show up well among deep greens, so complement with light greens, whites, yellows.
Purple, Violet	Royal, sensual, mysterious, intellectual, contemplative, creative. May be solemn, the liturgical color for Lent.	Darker shades need a lighter background to show up well. Complements yellow. Also try lighter shades, such as lavender.
White	Elegant, innocent, pristine. Suggests purity, peace, clouds, heaven.	Illuminates the garden by reflecting any available light so that it can positively glow at twilight. Enhances other colors. Wonderful in shade but may appear washed out in full sun.
Gray	Calming, promotes creativity and thought.	Almost never seen in flowers but available in a variety of foliage plants. Good complement or buffer for many colors.
Pink	Gentle tenderness, sweetness, romantic, soothing, friendly.	Wide variety of shades from orangish salmon to purplish mauve don't always look good side-by-side. Separate with green, white, or other pastels. Dark and light shades can mix well.
Black	Brooding, mysterious. Suggests death. Can symbolize evil too. A novelty sought by a few.	Yes, there are some black flowers. Best used only as an accent. Will not be seen from a distance because they disappear into the shadows.

Scent and Sound

The best gardens are multi-sensory. When you buy plants that are in bloom, check to see whether the flowers have an attractive scent. If they are not in bloom, sometimes the plant tag will tell you if a particular variety is fragrant. Aromas are not limited to flowers. Herbs can add appealing smells to a garden. Do you remember a plant you loved to smell as a child? Be sure to include one or more in your garden, and it will bring back memories and feelings in a way that nothing else can.

Sounds can also help your mood in the garden. A friend of ours remembers being stuck in a traffic jam but actually enjoying the experience because of the unexpected chorus of frogs in a nearby field. When you encourage wildlife in your garden, you can hear birds, insects, and maybe even frogs or toads. Introduce the sound of running water for relaxation. It can be anything from a large waterfall with a recirculating pump to a small tabletop fountain.

The wind can bring pleasant sounds to your garden as it rustles the trees or tall ornamental grasses that you may have planted. Manmade wind chimes come in many sizes and materials. You may choose the soft sound of bamboo, a low-pitched chime, or a high bell-like sound. The bell-like chime might remind you of the movie *It's a Wonderful Life*, when it was said that, "Every time a bell rings, an angel gets his wings."

Chapter 14
Paper Gardens

The scale drawing is an indispensable tool for the landscape architect and a valuable one for the amateur gardener. Although we have seen beautiful gardens that the gardeners made up as they went along, many gardeners also find it helpful to draw a scale version of their property and map out future improvements on paper. The process is not overwhelming if taken step by step.

Existing Conditions

When you decorate a room inside your house, one of the first things you do is measure. You bring the dimensions of the floor to the carpet store and the window measurements to the drapery shop. When you buy a sofa, you know whether the place you want to put it will accommodate a love seat or a queen-sized sleeper sofa. The same considerations apply to a garden and should be no harder to accomplish.

Measure the dimensions of your yard including the outline of the house, and make a drawing on graph paper. For an easy homemade measure, take a piece of non-stretchy string several feet longer than the longest dimension of your yard, and tie knots at one-foot intervals. This will be good enough to measure in half-feet or third-feet, which is about as precise as you need to be on a large lot.

When you draw a diagram of a room indoors, you indicate the location of things like electrical outlets, windows, doors, etc. You don't want that new sofa to block a heating vent. Do the same thing in the drawing of your yard. Show the location and size of walks, terraces, utilities, immovable plants, and the doors and windows of your house. You have now made a sketch of Existing Conditions (see illustration). Make about a dozen photocopies to play with.

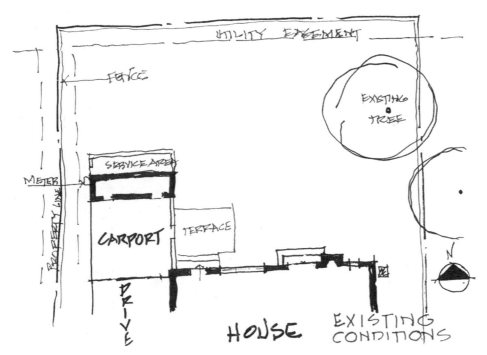

Visual Analysis

Now go for a walk through and around the entire area. If you are continuing to think of the garden space as a room to decorate, think about its "windows." Inside a house, if a window offers an appealing view, you select window treatments that frame the window, attracting your attention and encouraging you to look out. If the view is unattractive or you need privacy, you try for window coverings that meet the need without giving a sense of being closed in.

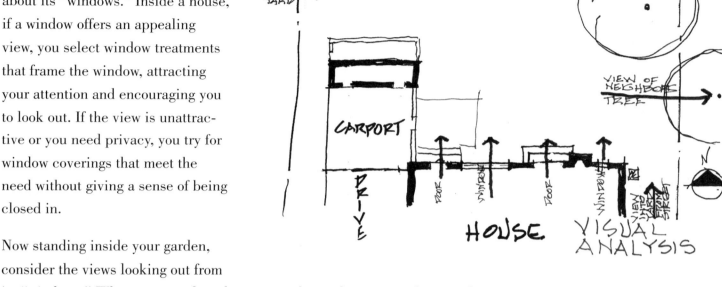

Now standing inside your garden, consider the views looking out from its "windows." When you stand on the terrace, do you have an unobstructed western view? You might imagine an arched trellis silhouetted against a sunset. Is there a bare wooden fence to the north? A pretty tree in your neighbor's yard to the east? A big, gray air-conditioning compressor next to your house to the south? When you stand at the gate, do you see your neighbor's flowering dogwood or his garbage can?

Then from the outside, looking in, consider all of the possible views of your garden. When you began, you might have wanted a place that would look pretty from the driveway and from inside your living room. Now think about all the other vantage points as well. How do you look into the garden from the kitchen window, from the carport, the street, the back door, and the bedroom window? Think about both privacy and visibility. You may be eager for passersby to get a glimpse of your prize irises, or you'd prefer a private spot where you can "draw the curtains." You can even plan for some of each.

Draw these observations on one of your diagrams (see Visual Analysis illustration). Some designers use straight arrows (in and out) to indicate good views and crooked arrows to indicate bad views. Landscape architects sometimes use shaded arrows or cross-hatched arrows.

Site Analysis

On another diagram, make notes of where water might stand after a heavy rain or during a rainy time of the year. Where does the ground slope and which way? Is the slope steep or gentle? Where is the flattest area that might be the easiest place for flower beds? The idea is to get everything that is in existence onto a piece of paper (see Site Analysis illustration). You can refer to the visual and site analyses when you begin sketching your plans.

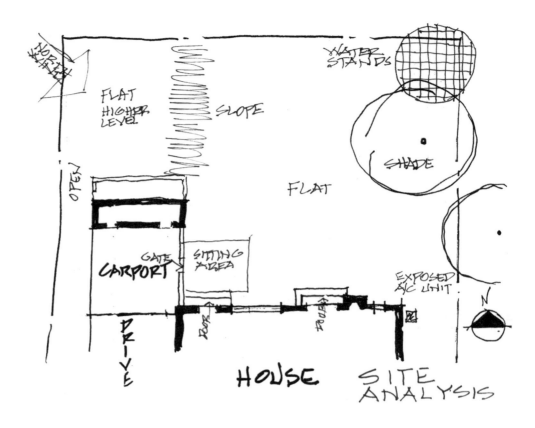

List of Desires/Needs

The next step is to make a wish list. Start with your general goals.

When Charles designed a memory garden for Lindenwood Christian Church in Memphis, the committee gave a list of preferences. They wanted the garden to be "elegant but not overdone" and to complement the building and existing structures. They wanted a meditative garden with places to sit so that they could conduct sunrise services there. Memorials would take the form of flat plaques. Engraved bricks would be sold to help fund the project. A statue or statues in the garden would recall the life of Christ or some event in His life. Good lighting, handicap accessibility, and minimum maintenance were also listed as important. The list was specific enough to help establish priorities but also flexible on some details.

Remember to base decisions on what you really want, not on what you think you ought to do. If you have specific items that you want to place in the garden, list them. Katie's classmates at Alcoa Elementary wanted a deck, a covered bench, a bird bath, butterfly houses, paths, and a fence. They also compiled a long, detailed list of flowers including butterfly bush, purple coneflower, daisies, zinnias, and others. Do you want a water feature like a fountain or a pond? Put it on your list.

Some of the wishes on your list can be fulfilled right away, while others will develop over time, and still others will languish on the list until you decide you really didn't want them anyway. At this point, the list helps you begin to bring some ideas into focus.

Preliminary Sketches

The emphasis here is on preliminary. Take the copies of the existing conditions and start doodling. Don't get hung up on precision and line quality. You might even try using crayons instead of pencil if it releases a childlike creativity for you. Just draw a rough circle to represent a piece of statuary or a square to represent a sitting area or a rectangle for a planting bed (see Preliminary Sketch 1, 2 and 3). Some people refer to this step as the "bubble" step because the forms you draw now are no more precise than bubbles.

Now put the sketch aside, and start another one. You may have five or six or more sketches by the time you get through. The biggest mistake most beginners make is to get too specific too

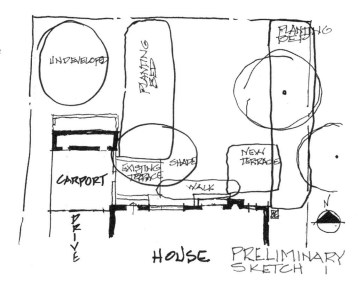

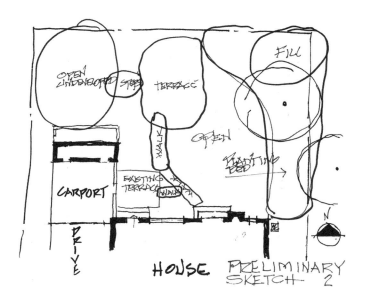

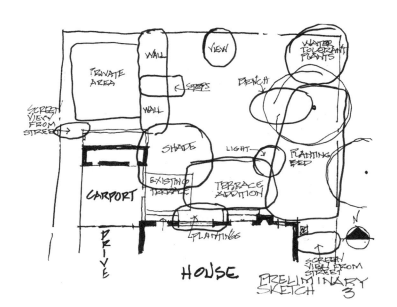

soon, such as selecting specific plants and then trying to force everything else to work around the first idea. Be free and open minded. Each sketch will stimulate additional ideas and help to fine tune your thought processes.

Shape the Spaces

Take a breather, and then select your favorite sketch. Connect the small, individual bubbles into larger, flowing forms. Ease out sharp angles and tight curves. Soften straight lines with gentle curves (unless you are designing a geometric, formal garden). Your sketch will begin to look pretty messy at this point, so copy or trace this new design on a fresh sheet of paper (see illustration).

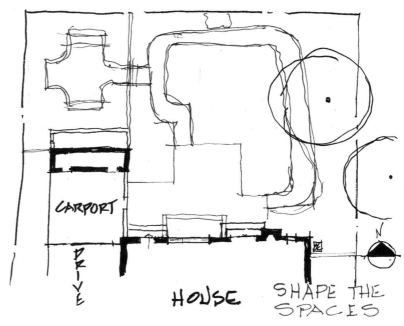

CARPORT

DRIVE

HOUSE

SHAPE THE SPACES

Work Out the Details

At this point, you will be ready to draw a plan that shows more exactly how you want your garden to look. Your sketch will not have the detailed information that a landscape architect's formal plan will have, but it will be extremely useful in making estimates. If your drawing shows exactly how wide that path will be and what route it will take, the salesman at the gravel company can tell you how much material you will need to construct it. When your sketch shows that you want a tree with a mature spread of 20 feet, the nurseryman can recommend varieties that will meet this requirement. If you want lighting, the electrician will be able to estimate the cost for you because your sketch shows him approximately how much wiring he will need from the nearest electrical source.

Your sketch can also help you plan phases of implementation for your garden, digging one bed this year, constructing the path next fall, and digging another bed the next spring. Years from now, you will keep referring to that old sketch to congratulate yourself on your progress and to remind yourself of other things you still want to accomplish.

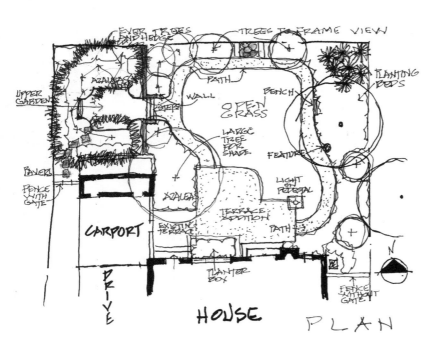

EVER TREES AND HEDGE

TREES TO FRAME VIEW

AZALEAS

PATH

WALL

OPEN GRASS

BENCH

PLANTING BEDS

UPPER GARDEN

STEPS

LARGE TREE FOR SHADE

FEATURE

PAVERS

FENCE WITH GATE

AZALEAS

LIGHT ON PEDESTAL

CARPORT

EXISTING TERRACE

TERRACE ADDITION

PATH

DRIVE

PLANTER BOX

FENCE WITHOUT GATE

HOUSE

PLAN

Chapter 15
Transplanting and Propagating Heirloom Plants

Uncle Ray suggested that every family member take some cuttings from Helen's garden before the family home was sold. Joyce took rosemary, and in spite of her lack of experience, it took root in her garden as a living remembrance of her mother.[1]

When you want to grow the same plant in your garden that was once in a loved one's garden, there are two approaches you can take. You can move the entire plant to your garden (transplanting), or you can take a part that will grow into a new plant (propagation).

Propagation is usually very easy. It is also guilt-free, because you are not depriving the original site of the plant. There are two basic types of propagation: seed (sexual reproduction) and vegetative (asexual reproduction). A disadvantage with seeds is that uncontrolled (open) pollination can produce a seed that won't grow to be exactly like the mother plant. Vegetative propagation produces more reliable results because you are cloning the parent plant. Cloning in the plant world is nothing new. If you can remember seeing bits of greenery stuck in jars on your grandmother's windowsill, you have seen vegetative propagation.

Seeding is also slower than vegetative propagation, and you can only collect seeds at certain times of the year. In a pinch, you can vegetatively propagate a plant at almost any time of year. You will have to rely on seeds for annuals, but for perennials, try some of the most common types of vegetative propagation: division, layering, or cuttings.

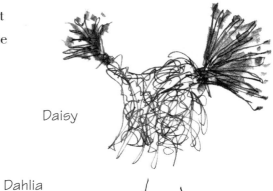

Daisy

Division

Division is the most foolproof form of propagation for herbaceous (soft-stemmed) perennials because you take away a small, intact plant. All the parts that it needs to thrive – root, stem, and leaf – are there. As perennials grow older, they spread into large clumps with baby plants around the edges. Often the crowded center of the clump becomes less produc-

Dahlia

Iris

77

tive and may even die. When you find this sort of doughnut shaped cluster of plants, you know without a doubt that you are doing the plant a favor by dividing it.

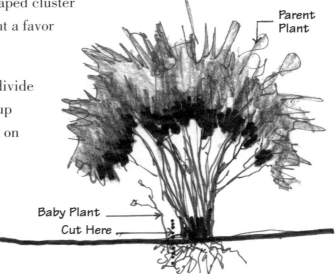

Parent Plant

Baby Plant
Cut Here

If possible, water the plant the day before you plan to divide it so that the soil will be soft and the plant well hydrated. Dig up the whole clump as if you were going to transplant it all. Lay it on its side on a tarp or an old sheet, and see whether the individual plants can be worked apart easily with your fingers. You can wash away some of the soil to make this easier if you are going to replant or pot the divisions right away. If you can't get the sections apart with your fingers, cut them apart with a sharp tool. You will lose a few small roots and stems in the process, but don't worry because a lot of the plant will be expendable.

Plants like hostas have a more dense, fleshy root system. This sounds brutal, but slice it. Dig up the whole clump. Put your cutting tool (a shovel, a knife, or even a saw) between groups of stems, and cut down through the root. Each division will dependably produce a new plant as long as you have included some root and attached stems.

You can choose to take many small divisions or only a few large ones. Larger divisions will become mature, flowering plants sooner, but small ones may be more easily transported and come in greater numbers. If the center of the parent plant has gotten old and woody, discard it and plant one of the young divisions in its place.

If the center is still relatively young, you may not need to dig up the whole plant. Simply put your shovel between the main plant and some baby plants, digging up only the babies and leaving the center undisturbed. Fill in with soil where you took the young plants out.

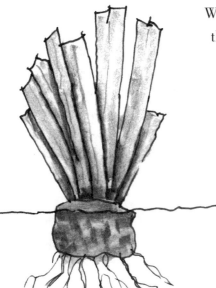

With very few exceptions, you should plant the divisions so that their crowns are at the same depth as the original plant. The best way to transport a baby plant to its new home is planted in a pot of dirt. The plants will almost invariably droop, but a drink of water will revive them. Keep them well watered until they become established.

Although it is feasible to divide perennials or transplant entire plants at almost any time of year, the least traumatic times for the plant are usually in early spring and early fall. The new growth is still small in the spring, but it is also vigorous and ready to start growing. In late summer or early fall, after the work of flowering, new plants have time to adjust and start establishing new roots before cold weather comes.

If your only chance is during the peak of the growing season, go ahead and divide. Cut back about two-thirds of the top growth so that the plant can turn more of its energy into reestablishing its root system. If you must divide during winter, divide the dormant plant, plant the divisions, and add some protective mulch. Even in winter, it is important to keep new plants well watered.

Bulbs, such as daffodils, use another type of division. The best time to divide is when the foliage is turning yellow after blooming. However, you can divide them any time you can find them. Dig up the clump and gently separate the smaller bulbs from around the central bulb. Replant at about the same depth or a little lower. If the plant is in bloom, cut off the flowers and enjoy them in a vase, but try to leave the greenery that will help to feed the bulb. Bulbs can be replanted immediately, or they can be stored (with leaves removed) in a cool, dry place until the usual planting time (autumn for spring-flowering bulbs and spring for summer-flowering bulbs like gladiolus).

When bulbs go year after year without division, they get crowded, smaller, and less productive. Eventually you get a clump of leaves trying desperately to feed a pack of tiny bulbs that can't muster a single flower. After division, it may take a year or two for the little bulbs to grow in size enough to flower, but they will in time. The bulbs you leave behind will benefit the same way, another example of why propagation is guilt-free.

Layering

If you don't have to hurry (as you might if a family home were being sold), you can get healthy young plants by layering. Shrubs and vines take especially well to this method of propagation. Layering offers the advantage of producing a young plant while it is still attached to the parent and can get the parent's nutrients.

Find a low-growing branch and bring it down to the ground. You can rough up the outer bark slightly where the branch meets the ground to stimulate the cambium, the layer of cells that will produce a new root. Bury the branch (still attached to the parent plant) about one-half inch deep. If it tries to spring back up, you can anchor it with a bent wire or even a brick. Keep the area moist but not soggy.

The best time to layer is in early summer. Depending on how woody the stems are, it may take a few weeks to a year for the new plant to be ready to live apart from its parent. After that, you can cut the "umbilical cord" and dig up the youngster for transplanting. Layering is such a natural form of propagation that you can sometimes find young plants near an older one where layering has occurred on its own.

If the plant you want to layer is not flexible enough to bend to the ground, you might try your hand at air layering. Surround a bud or leaf joint with moist rooting compound and hold it in place with plastic wrap and twine. When new roots have formed, cut the rooted branch away from the original plant.

Cuttings

It was probably 40 years ago, but Catherine still remembers when "Miss Bess" showed her and her father the old-fashioned, miniature pink rose. "Oh, just pinch off a piece, stick it in the ground, put a Mason jar over it, and it'll take root," said Miss Bess. She had just described the basics of propagation from stem cuttings.

Leave 2 leaves

Remove 1/2 of leaf

Remove all other leaves

Cut just below leaf node

You can root stem cuttings outdoors in the ground or indoors in trays. Although your grandmother may have rooted cuttings in water, the roots formed in a soil-type medium (see Chart 15.1) will be stronger than those grown in water. Prepare the soil where you will be rooting your cuttings so that you will lose no time getting the fresh cuttings into the medium. Softwood cuttings are taken in the spring, and hardwood cuttings in the fall. You can take cuttings at other times of year, although spring and fall are best. You may want to dip cuttings in root stimulate which is available at

garden centers, but this is not essential. If you are planting outdoors, choose a shady spot where the cuttings will get indirect light.

For softwood cuttings, clip a length of stem that includes several leaf nodes. Remove the leaves closest to the cut. If the stems are flexible, make a pilot hole in the medium with a pencil. Put the stems into the holes deep enough to cover one or two bare leaf nodes. Press the soil snugly around the cuttings to provide support. The top leaves will feed the cutting until the roots begin to form and work.

Moisten the soil well, but don't get it soggy. Construct a mini-greenhouse for your cuttings. It can be that Mason jar, a tent of plastic wrap supported by sticks, or a plastic milk jug with the bottom cut out. It is important that it not be in direct sunlight because it can become a solar oven there. In the shade, it will keep your seedlings warm and moist. Try to keep the leaves from touching the sides of the greenhouse, which can cause water to condense on the leaves and encourage fungus or rot. New roots may form as early as two weeks. You can check by gently tugging on the cutting.

Hardwood cuttings are easier but take longer. After fall dormancy has begun, cut several healthy branches in pieces five to ten inches long. Make sure a leaf node is near each end. Bundle them with string, make a trench in the garden, and lay the bundle on its side. Cover with moist sand. That's it. By spring there should be calluses on the cuttings. Plant each cutting with its callus in the soil. The hardest part is patience, because it may take years to have a full-sized plant this way.

Sometimes plants that have spreading roots lend themselves well to root cuttings. Dig up some pieces of these roots, and treat them much the same way you treat softwood stem cuttings. Let one-fourth inch show above the top of the soil, and be sure you plant them right side up, the way they were growing before you cut them. If you aren't sure, just plant enough so that the law of averages will work in your favor.

Seeds

For reasons mentioned earlier, seeding is our least favorite method for propagating perennials. It can work well for old varieties that are not hybrids. For annuals, the only means of propagation is seed, which is

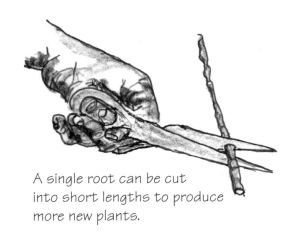

A single root can be cut into short lengths to produce more new plants.

81

the annual's reason for flowering in the first place. We also enjoy those plants that reseed themselves, naturally providing you with baby plants to move to your own garden.

Collect seeds when they are mature. The flowers will be faded and dry. Seed pods will open easily. When fruits or vegetables are over-ripe, you can collect their seeds. Clean the seeds, make sure they are dry, and store them in marked envelopes in a cool, dry place. Seeds vary in their requirements, but you are usually safe planting them outdoors after the danger of spring frost is past.

You may also want to start some seeds indoors about six weeks before they can be safely planted outdoors in the spring. Your biggest challenges will be to provide enough light and the right amount of moisture. A mini-greenhouse will help control temperature and moisture for sprouting. Clear, plastic deli containers work well as long as you cut drainage holes in the bottom. When seeds have sprouted, remove the lid from your "greenhouse." The best way to water seeds is with a mister, a spray bottle. This distributes a small amount of water evenly and gently without dislodging the seeds.

Even in a south window, the light may not always be enough to produce sturdy plants. If your seedlings are pale and spindly, you may need to use grow lights. Most large hardware stores carry the special bulbs that you can install in an inexpensive shop light. Suspend the light on lengths of chain so that you can adjust its height to stay a couple of inches above the growing plant. When the seedlings have developed their second set of leaves (the first pair of "true" leaves) they can be transplanted outdoors if it is warm enough for them.

Chart 15.1
Recipes for Rooting Medium

1/2 fine peat and 1/2 coarse, washed sand

or

1/2 perlite and 1/2 peat

or

1/2 perlite and 1/2 vermiculite

or

In the ground, add peat to lighten the soil and retain moisture.

Chapter 16
Selective Maintenance

One stitched sampler reads: "A garden is a thing of beauty and a job forever."

High maintenance? Low maintenance? No maintenance? Any discussion of maintenance involves balancing the garden's needs with the gardener's needs. What may seem like routine chores to the avid gardener may seem like high maintenance to someone else. Low maintenance for some people might leave the enthusiastic gardener complaining of nothing to do.

Only one thing is true for everyone: There is no such thing as no maintenance. Maintenance begins when the first plant is put into the ground and continues as long as you want to keep the garden. The basic needs for plants to grow are light, food, and water. If you provide for these needs, your memory garden will give you years of satisfaction. If you neglect them, the garden could become a source of frustration and guilt. The amount of work it takes to keep your garden in an orderly state can be tailored at least to some degree to fit your gardening personality.

The Sine Qua Non: Water

Sine qua non means "without which, nothing." Some plants do amazingly well with a minimum of care, but nothing, not even a cactus, can survive indefinitely without water. When actively growing, most plants require an inch to an inch and a half of water every five to seven days. For many weeks during the year, the rain takes care of that. Just remember to supplement when the rain is not doing its job. There are several options for watering including automatic systems, sprinklers or soaker hoses that you move around the yard, and hand watering. Daily, shallow watering is not good because it leads plants to produce

shallow, weak root systems. Deep watering on a regular, less frequent basis will encourage the plant to send its roots deeper into the ground, producing a stronger plant. It's less work for the gardener, too.

Some gardeners can almost eliminate the chore of watering by selecting drought-tolerant plants. Succulents like cactuses come to mind, but the selection is not limited to these. There are many books and articles available on xeriscaping (landscaping for drought tolerance). Many gardeners are attracted to native plants, the "wildflowers" that grow in a particular region and have adapted to the climate so that they can survive with little or no help from man.

If your garden includes some drought-tolerant plants and some thirsty ones, consider grouping them together according to their water needs. This way you can water those plants that need it without wasting water on plants that don't. For example, you may need to water impatiens twice a week, but you can skip some watering of the portulaca if it is in a different bed.

Feeding

You get the most results for the least effort when you fertilize your plants. Drop a little fertilizer into each planting hole as you put in the plant, and you will see improved results. Slow release fertilizers, such as Osmocote, will spare you numerous reapplications. Spray-on fertilizers, like Miracle Grow, help jumpstart a plant and may be repeated later in the season. Always follow instructions carefully to avoid chemical burning of the plant that can result from overdoing it.

Some gardeners make the mistake of assuming that withholding fertilizer will result in a slower growing plant and lower maintenance. That just gives you weaker plants. The way to have slow-growing plants is to select slow-growing varieties, not to underfertilize. A vigorous, well-fertilized plant can compete better against weeds and is less subject to disease and pests than an underfed plant.

Buy a fertilizer that is formulated for the use you want. Lawn fertilizers are high in nitrogen to produce lots of green leaves. You would not want to use a high-nitrogen fertilizer for flowers because the plant would produce an overabundance of leaves and fewer flowers. You can buy fertilizer based on its content (see Chart 16.1) or leave the chemistry up to the manufacturer and buy packages labeled "for lawns," "for flowers," etc.

Again, the most important rule is *follow the instructions*. Some products are made to be sprinkled on the ground as granules, but others are meant to be diluted with water. Don't assume that, if a teaspoonful gives good results, a tablespoonful will be ever better. You'll see this rule again when we discuss herbicides and insecticides.

Chart 16.1

Fertilizer

Symbol	Element	Function
N	Nitrogen	Stimulates top growth, deepens plant color, especially green plants
P	Phosphorus	Builds strong stems, strengthens root system
K	Potassium	Encourages a stronger, healthier plant, increases disease resistance

Weeding

Your plants can get a better allotment of light, water, and food, if they don't have to share these things with weeds. A weed is defined as any plant that is growing where you don't want it to be.

You can prevent weeds that grow from seeds by using a pre-emergent herbicide. These chemicals keep seeds from sprouting so that the weeds never appear at all. Apply them only if you are starting your garden with plants instead of seeds. Some of these herbicides are selective and will kill only broadleaf weeds or only grassy weeds. Others are not selective and will kill your marigold seeds as well as the chickweed seed. Read the label carefully.

You may also use a post-emergent herbicide that you spray directly on the unwanted plants. Again, some are formulated to attack only broad-leaf plants, others will attack only grasses, and some are non-selective. A non-selective herbicide, like Round-up, will kill any green plants it hits, so aim the spray carefully, and don't use it on a windy day when the spray is likely to scatter on the plants you want to keep.

If you have the patience to wait, use a broad-spectrum herbicide, such as Roundup, on the site of a proposed bed a week or two before you start to dig, so that the chemical has time to work. Then turn the soil for a bed that is totally free of any living weeds – at least for a while. Finally add pre-emergent herbicide to kill any weed seeds.

You will have to hand-pull some weeds later on, but many people actually enjoy this activity. If you can identify the weeds when they are young, they will be easier to pull. A vexing problem is that some weeds, in their young stages, can disguise themselves as the plants you are cultivating. Soon after planting astilbe, for example, we've seen a wild vine that starts out looking like young astilbe. When something like this happens, you just have to wait until the impostor is mature enough to identify and admire the weed's resourcefulness in the meantime.

If the thought of hours of weeding turns you off, you will be surprised at how much you can accomplish by just pulling a few handfuls every time you pass the garden. Be careful to confine this habit to your own garden. Certain plants that are weeds in your garden may be wild flowers in someone else's.

Pest and Disease Control

Gardeners are generally divided into two camps on pest and disease control: organic and non-organic. Whether you choose to avoid synthetic chemicals or not, there are some basic guidelines that apply. Take the following true-false test:

An ounce of prevention is worth a pound of cure.
> False. Avoid "preventive treatment." Don't spray bugs that aren't there. The presence of a few bugs does not constitute an infestation. If your plants remain healthy, don't upset the balance of nature.

A stitch in time saves nine.
> True. Inspect your plants when you do other tasks (deadheading, weeding, etc.) When you see plant damage, try to determine the cause and treatment before the problem becomes severe.

The only good bug is a dead bug.
> False. There are more beneficial insects than harmful ones. Some are essential for pollination of plants. Others feast on the harmful insects. Still others are just pretty to look at. Some provide food for birds. Those big, scary-looking garden spiders are helpful in keeping down harmful insects.

Don't drive a tack with an air-hammer.
> True. It is almost never necessary to spray your whole yard with a broad-spectrum chemical. Find out what kind of pest you have. Treat it as specifically as possible and only in the affected area. Your county agent or a reputable garden center can help you determine which treatments to use that will be effective with the least environmental impact. When you use insecticides, always follow the manufacturer's instructions carefully.

Treat plant diseases the same as insect problems. Try to get an accurate diagnosis, and treat as specifically as possible. If you know which diseases a particular plant is susceptible to, you are ahead of the game. Look for resistant varieties when you buy the plant, and provide a beneficial location for it. For example, tall phlox is prone to powdery mildew, but there are resistant varieties. Plant mildew-prone plants where air circulates well so that the foliage does not stay wet for long periods of time.

Some diseases in their early stages can be cured by simply cutting off and discarding the affected parts of the plant. Others require chemical treatment, such as a fungicide. When a disease cannot be cured, remove the plant entirely to prevent spread to the rest of the garden. Discard diseased plant cuttings. Do not compost them because this can perpetuate the problem.

Deadheading, Pruning, and Clean-up

Thriving plants eventually need some trimming. The most basic form of trimming is deadheading, which means to cut off old flowers that have passed their prime. This keeps the garden looking neat and also encourages growth of more flowers. Every flowering plant's main goal in life is to produce seed, so when you remove the old flowers, the plant is more likely to try again. Depending on what kind of flower you have, you might cut down to the next bud, the next large leaf cluster, or the entire flower stalk. At the end of the growing season, if you can tolerate a wilder look, you may decide not to deadhead, leaving seeds for birds to eat.

You can approach pruning shrubs in several ways. One neighbor keeps a fast-growing hedge in check with monthly trimming. Another cuts his hedge severely once or twice a year and then enjoys the birds that flit in and out of the somewhat scraggly bushes the rest of the time. A third neighbor digs up his hedge and replaces it with a slower growing alternative. All of these actions meet the same gardening need, but each one fits the kind of work that the gardener is more willing to do.

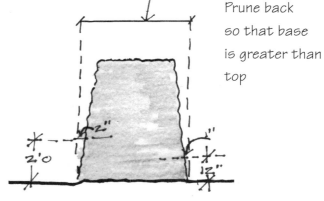

Prune back so that base is greater than top

Plant selection can help determine future pruning needs. Find out the expected mature size that a plant will reach and provide adequate room for it so that you will not have to prune it to keep it squeezed into a tight area. Buy a plant whose natural shape approximates the shape you want it to be. Don't try to make a sphere out of a plant that wants to be a pyramid.

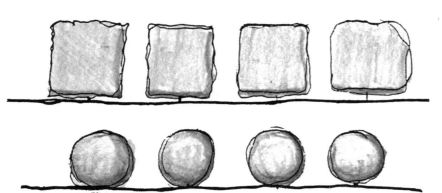

Shrubs should be trimmed in keeping with their natural shape, not artificial forms like these.

Most flowering shrubs look best when they are allowed to grow into their natural shape and size. If you must prune, do it soon after the plants bloom so that you don't cut off next year's buds. Instead of pruning to hard-edged forms, reduce the plant's size by cutting back only the longest branches.

After pruning or deadheading, remove the trimmings from the bed so that they will not rot on the ground and harbor pests or diseases. If the trimmings are healthy, you can compost them.

Mulch

Mulch is not a necessity, but it can be extremely helpful in a variety of ways. It regulates soil temperature, keeping it warmer in the winter and cooler in the summer. It helps to hold water in the soil beneath it and keeps mud from splashing on plants. It smothers weeds, and any weeds that take root later in the loose mulch will be easy to pull.

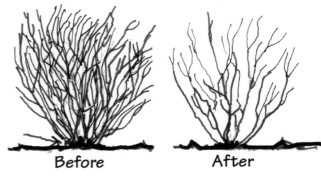

Before   **After**

Thinning Technique for Deciduous Shrubs
Remove about 1/3 of the oldest trunks.
Prune at or near ground level.

You can buy mulch by the bag or the truckload, but don't pile it more than about four inches deep. Some gardeners mistakenly pile mulch high around tree trunks, which can harm the tree by keeping the bark too damp and providing a haven for pests that enjoy munching on the bark under cover.

Add 2"-3" Pine Straw in the basin left by planting countractor

Also in barren areas under larger existing trees.

Never pile up leaves more than 3"± around trees

Some of the materials used for mulch include shredded wood, wood or bark chips, pine straw, cotton seed hulls, compost, and non-organic substances like gravel and crushed seashells. We prefer organic mulches because they are biodegradable. Although this means they have to be replaced more often, they can be dug into the soil to condition it, and they also control soil temperature better. One word of caution about using fresh wood products: the decomposition process requires nitrogen, so do not dig fresh wood mulch into the soil where it can rob your plants of the nutrient. Let it remain on top of the soil for a few years until it has broken down.

Plant Selection

You don't have to be an expert to enjoy a garden, but the more you know, the more you will be able to develop your garden and give it the appearance you want. When you select a plant, see how many of these questions you can answer:

- Is my soil sandy, loamy, or heavy clay?
- Is the yard mostly sunny, shady, or a combination?
- What light does this plant prefer?
- Does this plant fit my USDA cold hardiness zone and my AHS heat zone?
- How susceptible to pests and disease is this plant?
- How big will it be at maturity?
- What are its water requirements?

Even if you can only answer a few of these questions, this much knowledge will improve the plant's chances of thriving. Information about the plant is available on plant tags or in catalogs, or you can ask a knowledgeable employee at the garden center. Many good catalogs have toll free lines for questions about the plants they carry.

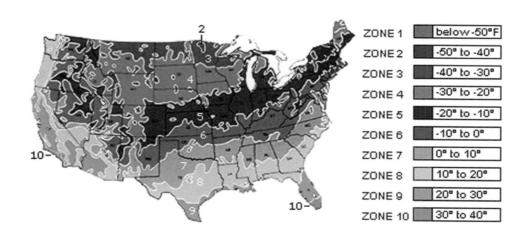

USDA Cold Hardiness Zone Map

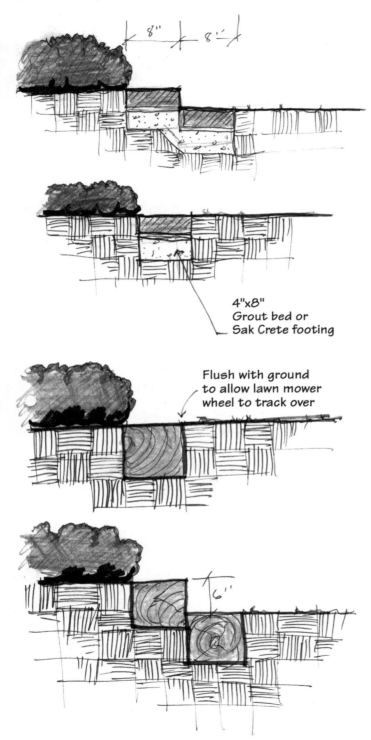

8" | 8"

4"x8"
Grout bed or
Sak Crete footing

Flush with ground
to allow lawn mower
wheel to track over

6"

Construction for Decreased Maintenance

Whole books have been written about low maintenance gardening, but here are two of our favorite tips.

Raised beds have the obvious benefit of reducing the amount of stooping you have to do to tend them. They are particularly useful in areas where the soil has a high clay content because they allow water to drain away instead of forming a "bathtub" that would promote root rot. Weeds that spread by runners have a little harder time stepping up into a raised bed.

Mowing strips eliminate the task of edging around your beds. Using the same material you used to enclose your bed (brick, stone, or timbers) sink another row of it in the ground just outside the bed. Your lawnmower wheels will roll over this row, allowing you to cut as close as you need to the bed. If weeds grow in the cracks or seams of your mowing strip, just spray with a vegetation killer like Roundup, and the problem is solved.

When you have arranged your memory garden so that its maintenance level harmonizes with your time and inclination, tending it will be a labor of love and not a chore.

Maintenance of Public Gardens

Many people who have established school gardens or other public gardens have shared with us the fact that it is relatively easy to get money and labor to build a garden, but it is quite another matter to get support for maintaining it. If the garden is a municipal garden, arrangements may be made in the planning stages for maintenance by city employees or a reliable corps of volunteers, such as Master

Gardeners. Schools often have a parents' club committee for grounds beautification. Katie's Garden is assisted by two garden clubs in the community.

You may decide to assume responsibility yourself, but be sure it really is your decision and not something that lands in your lap by default. A parent at one school told us of becoming very involved with his project at the beginning. His employer donated plants, which he helped tend for the first four years. Eventually, the responsibility for maintenance diminished to him alone. After a while, he became discouraged, and the garden began to decline. One day he went back to the garden after a long absence and had a chance meeting with another parent who also happened to be visiting that day. She discussed her plans to set up a fund to maintain the garden, and their enthusiasm was restored. He now tends the garden frequently and says, "I finally realized I was doing it for myself as much as for anyone else."

Afterword

We hope that you have already begun your garden and that we have given you the encouragement and information you need. May your garden thrive and lift your spirits. May the memory of your loved one always be associated with beautiful colors, lovely scents, and soothing sounds.

Although a garden cannot take the place of a loved one, we do believe that creating something beautiful in the natural world can provide great comfort while you wait for time to dull the pain of your loss.

May the words of the psalmist hold true for you:

"He that goeth forth and weepeth, bearing precious seed, shall doubtless come again with rejoicing, bringing his sheaves with him" (Psalm 126:6).

To Friends of the Bereaved

When a friend has lost a loved one, you often find yourself wondering, "What can I do?" It may help to suggest that your friend begin a small memory garden. Catherine's friend, Connie Scott, provided a great deal of support during Becky's illness and its aftermath. When she found out that Catherine was starting a memory garden, Connie shared divisions of plants from her garden. She placed no pressure on Catherine to use the plants but simply made them available to be used as Catherine saw fit. Several of those plants are still growing in or near the Becky garden.

Anastatia Fournet tells a completely different story, however, and asked that we share it with you. When her first baby died shortly after birth, he was buried at a small family cemetery. Because it was a private cemetery, the survivors were free to decorate the graves in any way they saw fit. Anastasia began to visualize a pretty garden at her baby's gravesite. It was several hours' drive from her home to the cemetery, so she took time to make sketches and to consider which plants would provide year-round color in her Louisiana climate. As she planned, she was comforted by the words to the old hymn, "I come to the garden alone, while the dew is still on the roses…"

The next time she was able to visit the grave, she discovered that another relative had already planted a garden there.

Ten years later, tears still came to Anastasia's eyes when she told us, "I knew she had meant well, but it was the only thing left that I could do for my child, and she took it away from me."

Encourage your grieving friend, but don't take the project away from him or her in your enthusiasm. If your friend does decide to begin a garden, the garden will give you many opportunities to ask how your friend is doing. It can be an opener to discussing how he or she is feeling, or it can be a "safe" topic of conversation that doesn't have to go any deeper. Just ask how the garden is coming, and your friend can determine where the conversation goes from there.

Although it is difficult for avid gardeners to imagine, there are some people who will not be interested in starting a memory garden. In those situations, the bereaved person will still appreciate it if you tell them you are doing something special yourself. One of Becky's nurses told Catherine, "Becky was so special to me, and I'll always miss her. I'm planting a pink dogwood in my front yard, and whenever I pass it, I'll think of sweet Becky." An expression like this will warm the heart, whether the mourner is a gardener or not.

Endnotes and Credits

Chapter 1

[1] Golden, Tom. "Fixing a Hole/Grieving With Other Men." Internet Column.

[2] Mandel, Rucy. Quoted in "Goodness Grows." *Better Homes and Gardens Garden Ideas & Outdoor Living* (Spring, 1997), 104-111.

[3] Shuchter, Stephen R. *Dimensions of Grief*. San Francisco: Jossey-Bass Inc., Publishers, 1986, page 96.

[4] Ecclesiastes 3:1,2 (KJV)

[5] Isaiah 40:6,8 (RSV)

[6] Manning, Doug. *Don't Take My Grief Away*. NY: Harper and Row, 1984.

[7] Handel's *Messiah*, No. 23 – Air for Alto. Text: Isaiah 53:3

[8] Goldberg, Diane. quoted in "Goodness Grows" *Garden Ideas & Outdoor Living*, Spring, 1997. Excerpted from audio cassette, *The Wisdom of Gardening: Conversations with Elders and Others*, 1996 by Connie Goldman Productions.

[9] "Wild in the Alley." *Garden Design* (Dec 96/Jan 97), pp 22-23.

[10] White, Jeanne. *Chicken Soup for the Mother's Soul*, Jack Canfield et al, pg 88, Health Communication Inc. 3201 S.W. 15th. Deerfield Beach, FL 33442-8190

[11] Warner, Charles Dudley. My Summer in a Garden. Quoted in Bartlett's Quotations, 14th ed.

[12] Proverbs 25:20 (NIV)

[13] Duncan, Isadora. *My Life* NY: W.W. Norton, Inc., 1995 (paperback reissue)

[14] Golden, Tom. "Fixing a Hole" Internet column.

[15] Martin, Laura. "Flower Gardening, U.S.A." *Better Homes and Gardens Flower Gardening*, Spring, 1999, pp 46-62.

[16] Goldberg, op cit.

[17] John 12:24, I Corinthians 15:36

[18] James 5:7-8 (NIV)

Chapter 2

[1] Bost, Carolyn. "Memorial Garden." *Birds & Blooms* April/May, 1999, pg. 16.

[2] www.gwaa.org has instructions for finding or beginning a Plant a Row ("PAR") program in your community.

[3] Hicks, Thomas. "Mae: Touched By Sanctity's Wing." *America.* Vol. 169, Issue 13, October 30, 1993, page 6.

[4] Wolfelt, Alan D. *Healing the Bereaved Child*. Fort Collins, CO: Companion Press, 1996.

[5] The authors are compiling an extensive list of plants with people's names, to be published separately.

[6] "A garden of love: Remembering Oklahoma City." Family Circle, September 17, 1996, pp 44-49.

Chapter 15

[1] McGreevy, Joyce. *Gardening by Heart; the extraordinary gift of an ordinary garden*. San Francisco: Sierra Club Books, 2000.

[2] This method will work with old-fashioned, non-hybrid roses but not with modern, grafted varieties which require more sophisticated methods.

Credits

The illustrations in this book are all by the hand of Charles Nolan Sandifer with the following exceptions:

ArtToday.com's public domain vault provided the illustrations on pages 14b, 26, 28b, 29, 35, 40, 46, 47, 48, 71, 83, 93. All used with permission.

Theda Fritz took the photos of the memorial garden in Oklahoma City (page 11) on May 27, 2001. Used with permission.

Catherine Chappell Lewis drew the illustration on page 23.

The map on page 89 was provided by the US Government. Used with permission.

Glossary

Accessories – Man-made objects placed in the garden. Examples include furniture, wind chimes, decorative pots for plants, etc.

AHS Plant Heat Zone Map – Prepared by the American Horticultural Society, this map shows how many days certain areas can expect temperatures over 86 degrees Fahrenheit. (See USDA Cold Hardiness Map).

Amendments – Anything added to the soil to improve its texture or fertility. Organic amendments include bark, manure, humus, and compost. Inorganic amendments include perlite, sand, and vermiculate.

Annuals – Plants that naturally live their full life cycle from seed to death in one year. Examples: marigolds, zinnias, petunias

Arbor – An overhead structure often covered with vines. May be made of lattice, metal, branches, or other materials.

Axis or axial – Regimented, geometric design creating a straight center line that focuses on a strong end point. Most common use is in large, formal, classical gardens. Generally symmetrical but can be asymmetrical.

Balled and Burlapped – Technique of wrapping the root ball and surrounding soil when transplanting a tree or shrub that has been growing in the ground instead of being container-grown. This is done to minimize shock to the plant. The burlap is tied at the base of the main stem or trunk of the plant. The string should be untied and the top of the burlap gently pulled back after the plant is securely in the ground.

Balance – The perception that the visual weight of objects on each side of an area are approximately equal. Balance can be symmetrical or asymmetrical.

Bare root – Plants that are shipped during the dormant season with no soil around the root system. May be used for small trees and shrubs, some perennials and ground covers, and roses.

Board and board – Wood fence where the planking is on opposite sides of the structural support in an alternating pattern.

Broadcasting – A method of scattering fertilizer or seeds over an area. (Although many people still toss by hand, a mechanical spreader gives more uniform coverage.)

Bulbs – In certain plants, an underground structure with leafy scales or layers. Stores nutrients for the next year's growth. The plants that grow from bulbs are sometimes referred to as bulbs and include daffodils, tulips, and onions. Often the term is loosely, though incorrectly, used to refer to similar underground structures such as corms, rhizomes, and tubers.

Circulation – The route(s) one uses to get from place to place in the garden.

Coherence – The blending together of a composition so that it is seen as a whole and not as a group of isolated elements.

Color – Reflected light from parts of the spectrum. Obvious in flowers but important also in leaves, stems, mulch, and man-made objects.

Composting – The process of collecting organic matter such as leaves, grass clippings, kitchen scraps, and manure from herbivores, and piling this matter in a place where it can decompose to a soil-like consistency that is rich in nutrients for plants.

Deadheading – Removing spent flowers, which encourages the plant to produce more flowers as it tries to produce seed.

Deciduous – Plants that shed all of their leaves at a given time (usually fall and winter) and then produce a new crop of foliage after a dormant period.

Evergreen – Plants that are never bare and which retain most of their foliage at all times. There is some shedding of leaves throughout the year. Examples include pine, holly, spruce and fir.

Fertilizer – Substance applied to soil or foliage to supply nutrients to plants. Fertilizers may be organic or inorganic. The three most important elements in fertilizer are nitrogen, phosphorus, and potassium. Three numbers appear on fertilizer packaging to indicate the proportions of these elements (in alphabetical order). For example, 5-10-10 fertilizer will have 5 parts nitrogen, 10 parts phosphorus, and 10 parts potassium.

Focal point – Article in the garden that attracts the greatest attention due to its striking nature. Other things in the garden are positioned so that they direct attention to it. May be a statue, structure, plant, water feature, or other significant object .

Form – Structural element of design that refers to the shape of the object or space. Forms include spherical, pyramidal, columnar, conical, oval, and vase-shaped.

Gazebo – Free-standing, roofed structure that is open on the sides and is used to take advantage of a view or to be a focal point of a garden.

Hardening off – Conditioning or acclimating a plant so that it can survive in a new environment. Typically, plants that are started indoors from seed or plants that have spent the winter indoors are placed outside in the spring for a few hours each day, increasing the time until the plant is accustomed to the outdoor environment.

Heeling in – Placing the root ball of a transplant in sand, bark mulch, or other medium for temporary protection when there is some reason that it cannot be properly planted immediately.

Humus – Dark, crumbly, soil-like substance that is the product of composting. Humus occurs naturally over the years on a forest floor. Available for purchase at many garden supply stores.

Lattice – Usually an open wood or wrought iron structure composed of geometric design(s), covering an area or used as a free-standing fence section. Often used to support vines, can be used as an overhead shade device or to partially screen out objectionable views.

Leaf mold – Compost derived from leaves only.

Line – Structural element of design that refers to the configuration of an object. For example, a fence may have a straight line, the edge of a planting bed may form a curved line, or the edge of a plant may suggest a line.

Mowing strip – A band of concrete, brick, timber, or other material placed flush with the ground just outside a planting bed so that a mower can roll over it to cut the edge of the grass. This major maintenance saving device also serves as a barrier to grass getting into the planting bed.

Mulch – Material used to cover the soil in planting beds to keep down weeds and regulate moisture and temperature. Organic mulches include shredded bark, bark nuggets, pine straw, cotton seed hulls, and compost. Inorganic mulches include black plastic, landscape cloth, and newspaper, all of which look better if covered by a layer of organic mulch. Some gardens, especially those featuring drought-tolerant plants, use gravel as mulch.

Native plants – Plants which occur naturally in an area. Use of native plants assures having a garden that tolerates the local climate, requires less fertilizer, and is environmentally friendly, often attracting a more diverse wildlife population.

Organic material – Substances derived from living organisms rather than synthetic chemicals. Usually kinder to the environment.

Orientation – How a visitor to the garden sees himself in relation to the location of features there. The relative position of the garden and its parts as seen from inside and outside its borders.

Parterre – Pattern on the ground usually defined by low hedge plants bordering and enclosing a seasonal display of garden color. Often a simple, symmetrical composition of shapes with paths in between. (French, from Old French, ornamental garden, from par terre, on the ground.)

Patio – Technically, an enclosed, paved terrace attached to the house and open to the sky. Term often used by laymen for any paved, recreational area, attached to the house and often used for outdoor dining.

Peat Moss – Dark, spongy, fine-grained soil conditioner. Excellent for acid-loving plants. Should be crumbled and moistened before use. Made from partially decomposed remains of any of several mosses. Sphagnum peat moss is generally highest in quality.

Perennials – Plants that live more than two years. Herbaceous (non-woody) perennials usually die back at the end of the season and put out new growth the next year. Examples: daisies, daylilies, irises.

Pergola – An overhead structure that is open on the sides with an arbor or lattice roof, supported by a series of parallel columns.

Perlite – Mineral that has been expanded by heating to form small, very lightweight, white balls. An excellent amendment for potted plants because of its light weight. Can also be used in planting beds, but the white pellets tend to look unnatural on the surface of the soil.

Pinching – Taking out the tips of new plant shoots to encourage the plant to form more side branches.

Plane – Flat, imaginary surface used in design to describe the placement of different elements. The base plane is usually the ground and is horizontal. The vertical plane may describe a hedge, fence, or walls. The overhead plane is horizontal and may refer to the sky, the tree cover, or the ceiling of a man-made structure.

Pocket garden – Small, intimate area adjacent to larger areas but screened off to give a secluded, private feeling. Usually designed for use by one or two individuals.

Post-emergent herbicide – Chemical product that is sprayed on actively growing vegetation to kill unwanted plants. Some are selective and are formulated to kill only broadleaf weeds (for use in a lawn) or only grassy weeds (for use in flowerbeds). Others are non-selective and will kill any green plant that they touch.

Potting "soil" – Mixture of organic and inorganic material, such as vermiculite or perlite. Sometimes does not include any actual dirt, making it lighter, better draining, and sterile.

Pre-emergent herbicide – Chemical product that prevents plant seeds from sprouting in a planting area. (Example: "Halts" crabgrass preventative.)

Principles – Abstract, general ideas which in garden design refer primarily to balance, scale, rhythm, contrast, unity, and harmony.

Proportion – The relative size of one thing to another.

Raised beds – Planting beds that have been elevated by mounding up or by use of retaining walls of brick, stone, railroad ties, etc. Provides better drainage and a more convenient height for working.

Scale – Relative size of objects in the garden (and the relative size of the garden itself) to the size of people using the area. The scale of towering redwoods can make us feel insignificant or filled with awe, while dwarf plants can give the feeling of being dominant or in control.

Scale drawing – A drawing in which measurements of the depicted area correspond proportionately with measurement on the drawing. Often a convenient scale for smaller areas is one inch on the drawing compared to one foot on the site. Larger areas may require one inch equal to eight feet.

Screening – Visually separating elements from each other. Examples: a hedge, lattice, fence, or wall.

Shearing – Overused practice of creating a uniform, level plant with hedge clippers. Should be used on formal, strongly symmetrical, geometric designs, but not on naturalistic designs.

Side dressing – Application of fertilizer on the ground in the root zone along the sides of plants.

Slow release – Usually refers to fertilizers that release their elements over a period of time. Less prone to burn plants. Requires fewer applications during the year.

Soil mix – Generally a garden soil that has been mixed with sand, peat moss, organic material, compost, or other soil amendment.

Species – Grouping of plants below genus but above individual varieties. In scientific nomenclature (e.g., Quercus alba) the first word refers to the genus, and the second word is the species. In this example, Quercus is the oak genus, and alba narrows it to the white oak species.

Sphagnum peat moss – Partially decomposed sphagnum moss. Often grayish and in a shredded form similar to fine spaghetti. Excellent for use in containers. Good for large planting beds, but more expensive than peat moss.

Terrace – Unenclosed, level surface which can be grass, inorganic materials (concrete, brick, gravel, etc.), or sometimes plantings. Also refers to the practice of taming a hillside by converting it to a series of level surfaces.

Texture – Structural element of design referring to the character of a surface, whether it is rough, smooth, coarse, fine, waxy, fuzzy, fibrous, etc. Can be perceived visually as well as tactically (for example, small leaves make a plant look fine-textured).

Topsoil – In undisturbed areas the top several inches of dirt that is most often rich with minerals and darker in appearance than the subsoil layers. Rarely is true topsoil found because of erosion and urban development where the soil has been graded. Most new gardens will need organic soil amendments and sometimes sand.

Trellis – Structural device designed to support climbing plants.

Unity – Principle that ties everything together into a whole composition. Can be a single dominating feature, such as a view of a mountain, or a repetition of elements like plant material, colors or construction materials.

USDA Cold Hardiness Map – Prepared by the United States Department of Agriculture, this map outlines zones based on winter low temperature ranges. Most plant tags list the zones in which a plant can be expected to survive the winter. (See AHS Plant Heat Zone Map.)

Variegated – Having multicolored foliage, which can be in the form of spots, colored edges, or stripes on the leaves.

Variety – Sub-classification of species, usually in quotation marks. (e.g., "Arthur" is a variety of delphinium, which is the species, Delphinium elatum.)

Vermiculite – Inorganic soil amendment from mica. Helps to lighten soil and hold water and air. More natural looking in beds than perlite.

Vistas – Views (e.g., mountain, valley, stream) that are framed by elements of the garden such as a row of shrubs or trees leading the eye to focus on the desired object. Used on a smaller scale in gardens to focus on features like a fountain or statue.